She Sells

Attract, Promote, and Retain Great Women in B2B Sales

By Lori Richardson

DEDICATION

This book is dedicated to the men and women in professional, B2B sales organizations who understand the power of what an inclusive sales team can bring and who work hard at it every day. It is also written for the women who left the sales profession for various reasons and for the women who did not feel at home in this amazing profession. This is for those who have built and/or run women in sales communities within their company or on their own and who have a commitment to equitable and inclusive sales teams worldwide.

Finally, for the rural public-school teacher, Mary, who left her $24K teaching position and got into an ed-tech SaaS sales role and is now making $100K+ after two years. The sales profession empowered her, gave her tools to better raise her family, and she supported her community in financial ways she never expected. To those who know how much a B2B sales career for a woman or those underrepresented can be a game changer and a life changer: this book is for you, too.

MANY THANKS

This book includes snippets, stories, and lessons from my journey to better understand why it hit me so hard that little had changed in sales and being around inclusive sales teams. At some point, I became numb or just accepted that I worked in a male majority world. Two female mentors helped me shed my numbness. Speaker and author Jill Konrath modeled great leadership and helped me find my own voice to launch Women Sales Pros; and Trish Bertuzzi, sales strategist and author of "The Sales Development Playbook," who commiserated with me when we saw yet another all-male panel or only men speakers at sales conferences. Jill and Trish, who are very competent and capable sales experts and sales thought leaders, female or male, taught me we are so much more than a gender label. We are valuable contributors to our industry.

I also want to thank all the Women Sales Pros members, past and present, with a special note of thanks to Joanne Black for all her work championing this cause, to my good friend, Alice Heiman who has been a sounding board, and my friend Barbara Giamanco, whose podcast, "Conversations with Women in Sales" I have carried on since she died in May of 2020. An additional shout-out goes to the advisory board members, including Jill, Trish, Colleen Stanley, Janice Mars, Jamie Crosbie, Julie Hansen, Lynn Hidy, Lisa Dennis, and Meshell Baker.

I'm continually inspired by corporate sales champions, including Mary Shea, Ph.D., Gavriella Schuster, Rakhi Voria, Hang Black, Anna Baird, Cate Gutowski, Amy Appleyard, Natasha Sekkat, Debbie Dunnam, Caitlyn Gill, and all the female executive sales leaders including C-level women.

Very special recognition goes to the great women championing the cause for inclusive sales teams who have also built or are building women in sales communities/groups/clubs and organizations/ events, including Chantel George, Lauren Bailey, Angela Salazar, Cynthia Barnes, Eva Helen, Alexine Mudawar, Gabrielle Blackwell, Cassie Yettru,

Alex Adamson, Heidi Solomon-Orlick, Roshni Baronia, Gina Stracuzzi, Deanna Ransom, Shari Johnston, Tracy Eiler, Lynn Powers, Debe Rapson, Chitra Singh, Lanette Richardson, Jessica Weiderhorn, Cindy Lien Truong, Thilaga Kumar, Ali Powell, Leigh Koritke, Shannon Hempel, Rana Salman, Thilaga Kumar and Ines Ben Brahim.

Big thanks to all of the women and men involved in "women in sales" groups at your companies. I've spent time with many, and some are mentioned in the book.

Male allies and colleagues in professional selling are far too numerous to mention. There are dozens and dozens of men I've worked with who have supported and encouraged me since I began in tech sales in the '80s, including Barry Kenney, Ed Scherer, Richard Johnson, and Joe Brown at The Byte Shop in downtown Seattle. In recent years, appreciation goes to some real standout supporters where we've had conversations, meetings, events, panels, and more, including Dr. Howard Dover for including women's voices in so many ways and Dr. Joel Le Bon for the research we began (and hope to complete). To Shep Maher and Ryan Bott for being corporate champions and contributing to a panel or conversation whenever you can, and Bob Perkins (and team) for making room for inclusion conversations at AA-ISP events. Thanks to Henry Schuck for your observation about women not even applying for sales roles (in the early years of DiscoverOrg) which got my wheels turning. Thank you. To Billy Bob Brigmon for your efforts at a corporation that didn't "get it," but we all learned so much. Thanks to Chris Mooney for our GAF Women in Sales project, where change has been visible. Thanks to my colleagues Dave Brock, John Barrows, Andy Paul, Tim Clarke, Scott Ingram and Ryan O'Hara. I can't name all the great men who listened and who tried new ways to help and become changemakers here. You know who you are.

Here are thanks to those in academia championing more women in sales and inclusive sales teams. There are so many of you, but I recognize here those I've had more interaction with: Joel Le Bon, Ph.D., Howard Dover, Ph.D., Jane Sojka, Ph.D., Stefanie Boyer, Ph.D., Robert M. Peterson, Ph.D., Semiramis Amirpour, James McIlroy, and Marty Holmes with the SEF.

This book was a long time coming, so a thank you first to Barbara Weaver Smith for helping me kick it off and thank you to editor extraordinaire M. Sharon Baker for her tireless work and suggestions. Thank you to the book "team" and to Doug Eymer of Eymer Brand Laboratories & Think Tank for the design, layout, and magic of putting it all together into Kindle and print. Thanks to the early readers.

Thank you, Peter, for sticking by my side throughout this lengthy process, and last but not least, thanks to the rest of the Score More Sales and Women Sales Pros team, clients, and community for your support.

TABLE OF CONTENTS

FOREWORD

BY JILL KONRATH

If it wasn't for Xerox, I wouldn't be where I am today as a top sales expert with four best-selling books and more than 375,000 followers on LinkedIn.

It all started when Xerox hired me in 1978. They were one of the first and very few companies to make a concerted effort to hire women and minorities in sales. Leadership supported the initiative. After some initial hiccups, they figured out how to do it right. In fact, in hindsight, they pretty much followed Lori's playbook.

Initially, many of the tenured Xerox salesmen had doubts that women could sell "machines." They were also concerned about our credibility with buyers. They were wrong.

By the time I arrived on the scene in 1978, women were 50% of Xerox's sales force. In many regions, they were at the top of the leaderboards. But as I moved on to other organizations, I learned just how unique Xerox was.

Despite Xerox's pioneering efforts in hiring women, today, most sales organizations are still male-dominated with strong "bro" cultures. It's a natural human tendency to hire people who are like you. They're in your comfort zone.

But is it a wise business decision?

As Lori points out in She Sells, numerous studies show that women in sales outperform their male colleagues—by a respectable amount. Think about it. As a sales leader, meeting your numbers could be a whole lot easier.

Additionally, data shows that female sales reps stay in their jobs longer. As a sales leader, that means you won't have to source, interview, and onboard so many new hires. Nor will you have to wait months till they finally reach quota.

Here's my big question for you:

If hiring women can have such a positive effect on your team's performance, why isn't it one of your primary strategic initiatives?

Sure, you have to do things differently—just like when you tackle any new endeavor. But it's worth it. And She Sells gives you the blueprint needed to make it a reality.

I've known Lori for more than 15 years. A passionate advocate for women in sales, she's spearheaded research on what it takes for them to succeed. She's spoken at numerous conferences, and now she's written the definitive book.

Now it's up to you. Go get 'em!

Jill Konrath
International speaker and author of *Selling to Big Companies*,
SNAP Selling, *Agile Selling*, and *More Sales Less Time*

CHAPTER ONE

Why This Book Now

"What great changes have not been ambitious?"

MELINDA GATES

Introduction

I'll never forget the time that I finally met a big group of sales managers that I'd previously only seen individually in their offices up and down the East Coast. These sales managers, over 80 total, represented a privately-held billion-dollar telecom company. Our big group session was about to begin.

When I walked in, I scanned the room, and suddenly I saw everything differently. All of these managers (and their managers) I had been working with over time were now here in one space. The room was nearly all men. Young, old, and in-between white men.

I counted only four women sales managers in the group of 80. That is the very moment it hit me and launched me on my journey to help create inclusive sales teams. I was stunned. I thought, "Where are the women?" These weren't technical positions but general sales manager roles.

I didn't say anything that day, but from then on, I knew I had to find out why, in 30+ years' time, there were still so few women on my clients' sales teams and especially in sales leadership. I don't only work in telecom but also in software, tech, manufacturing, distribution, and financial services.

Countless studies, publications, and people have noted the lack of women in sales and women in leadership positions. Consider that there has been little research on women in sales roles and women in sales leadership roles. I'll share here what I have observed in recent years.

Are women underrepresented in sales? YES

According to Forrester's research (Jan 2021), women represent less than one-third of B2B (business-to-business) sellers and one-fourth of B2B tech sales roles. Women hold 12% of top sales leadership roles.

Gartner reported in 2018 that "the sales function has the second biggest gender equity gap of all corporate functions."[1]

In 2019, DiscoverOrg (now Zoominfo) updated its 2016 Gender Diversity[2] study, and the data about women in sales leadership roles is disheartening. The study looked at Women Leaders by Department 2019, defining "leaders" as women with titles of VP, Executive VP, Senior VP, or President. They found these percentages of women leaders by department:

Human Resources	68%
Marketing	42%
Legal/Compliance	45%
Information Technology	27%
C-Suite	18%
Sales	14%

Sales are in a dismal last place. The same study found only 11% of women in the Chief Revenue Officer role, down 15% from 2016. The 2018 Gartner study showed women at 19% in sales leadership, almost equally as bad.

Do women succeed in sales? Also, YES.

In contrast to the data about the numbers of women in sales, we know that based on every study available, as a group, women do well in sales.

McKinsey reported in 2021 that company profits are close to 50% higher when women are well-represented at the executive level.

Gong Research Labs conducted a study in 2017 in which they analyzed 30,469 B2B recorded and transcribed sales calls made by both women and men.[3] The data set was slightly skewed towards men (17,000+ male and 12,000+ female), but they constructed a statistically significant set of calls to analyze, including similar industries and deal sizes.

They were surprised to find that women listened slightly less, interrupted twice as often as men, and went on longer monologues. However, women closed deals at a higher and faster rate than men in this study; on average, women had an 11% higher win rate than men.

Xactly Insights data shows that women have median quota attainment 8% higher than their male counterparts. Also, teams led by women tended to have a higher win rate and quota attainment (94%) compared to male-led teams (91%)

So, if women perform and lead better, Xactly wondered why sales is still a male-dominated field. They consider it primarily a matter of unequal compensation:

"Although women perform higher and are paid out at a slightly higher median commission rate (2.13% for women vs. 1.30% for men), their total compensation is still lower than male reps. On average, women earn only 77% of the total compensation male sales reps earn ($120,732 vs. $156,012)."[4]

Dr. Joel Le Bon was the Director of the University of Houston, Bauer College of Business, Stephen Stagner Sales Excellence Institute, as well as a marketing and sales professor teaching a Sales CRM class. He conducted a study using a database of the performance of his 1,042 sales students (47% men, 53% women) during 16 semesters from 2010 through 2018.

The students had a sales challenge assignment. In his article, *Who are the Sales Superheroes?*[5], Professor Le Bon reports, "They had to sell openings for players and sponsorships for the PES Open. Their sales quota was $800 ($500 for a foursome + $300 for golf sponsorships). The students received a sales territory of about 250 accounts and had eight weeks to learn Social CRM technologies and sell the golf tournament. If they didn't make their sales quota, the likelihood for them to pass the class was quite low." Here are the results he reported:

Since 2010, and from a sales volume standpoint, the sales students have sold a total of 8,745 players, averaging 547 players per golf tournament.

From a sales revenue standpoint, they have sold for a total of $1,990,984.31, averaging $1,924 of sales per student.

Since 2010, 7 Top Producers have been men, and 10 Top Producers were women!

Together, the alumni men Top Producers have sold for a total of $74,572, averaging $10,653 per sales student. (std. dev.: $4,295)

Together, the alumni women Top Producers have sold for a total of $113,412, averaging $11,341 per sales student. (std. dev.: $9,039)

Yet in 8 years, and regarding Top Performers, we had 58.8% more 'WonderSalesWomen' than 'SuperSalesMen'!

*And '**WonderSalesWomen**' have outperformed 'SuperSalesMen' by 52%!*

So, if women are successful in sales, why aren't there more of them?

After doing hundreds of interviews, conversations, webinars, and panels, my answer is: it's complicated.

There is not one single issue to just "turn around" and fix. It is a series of elements, including the environment of sales, the baggage sales carry as a profession, a lack of awareness of the profession, the relative lack of standout female role models, and women themselves, that make for this concoction of failure so far.

I call it: The Women in Sales Conundrum.

Its components include:

Barriers to attracting women to sales:

- Socialization of girls toward other occupations
- Negative stereotypes of salespeople and sales as a career
- Shortage of visible female role models in sales
- Most U.S. colleges & universities do not have a sales program (SEF schools listed here https://salesfoundation.org/SEFAnnual/), yet many women want a degree to feel more prepared (for example: the predominance of women in marketing vs. sales)
- It is a "hidden" career – many women have not heard of B2B sales opportunities

Barriers to hiring women into sales:

- Conscious and unconscious bias against women (and anyone different)
- Hiring for "culture fit"
- Characterization of sales positions exclusively in terms of male attributes, e.g., aggressive "killer" instinct
- Poor job conveying policies of parental (esp. maternity) leave specific to sales roles where there are quota issues, ramp-up issues, and deal-sharing issues
- Women don't know about the opportunities in B2B sales

Barriers to retaining women in sales:

- Bro culture of some sales teams, especially in tech/SaaS —aggressive, male-majority
- Unequal pay for women common
- Unequal and sometimes biased treatment by sales managers and colleagues
- Lack of female colleagues, executives, and sales leaders
- Unclear career path and cronyism in promotions

Despite the conundrum, there are individuals and companies that are making great efforts to bring more women into sales and seeing real results. This book is about how you can do the same in your company. I will show you how to build a foundation for change, how to find great women sellers, how to properly train them, when to promote them, and most importantly, how to retain them. You must do the heavy lifting to make it a reality, but I'm sure you'll be amazed at the results.

Here's the executive summary of what needs to happen:

Company leaders need to do their part:

- Have sales teams that are professional workplaces with understood professional development options, the right benefits, and an environment for all to thrive
- Understand how to find, attract, hire, and onboard more innovatively than the same old way some companies have done for years in sales
- Promote and professionally develop more women sales leaders

The sales community needs to do its part:

- Create more visibility for the profession of B2B sales and work to eliminate the old negative stereotypes
- Talk up successful women sellers and sales leaders in podcasts, videos, and at industry sales events
- Stop using "war words," sports analogies, and constant "hustle" to describe the sales process, sales teams, sales efforts, and sales in general

Women need to do their part:

- Be open to the opportunity of professional selling and bringing your personal style to the role

- Support other women within your team, your company, and outside of your company to encourage more women sellers and sales leaders

- Step up and speak up to gain promotion, be a role model, be visible, and make positive change happen

Some of you are on board with me already. I've heard your feedback. You are nodding, with wry smiles and a few grimaces. You are women and men in sales, sales management, and in corporate leadership. You've been here, facing these issues, maybe fighting for change, maybe struggling silently. Thank you for that. Perhaps you are as puzzled as I am and as frustrated as I am on some days. If you've been following this effort for a while, I'm going to give you a next-step exercise to stand up for more women in sales; more about this later.

Some of you are pushing back. I can sense your feedback too. I hear it often. You are women and men in sales as well. You are men who are tired of hearing this story. Wondering why it matters. Not interested. A few of you are outraged. Some of you are worried. If sales is more welcoming to women, will the profession be less welcoming to men? Others try not to think about #MeToo, afraid of making a mistake or being tossed out on a bad call. Some of you are women, highly successful in your sales career. You don't have any problems, and it's hard for you to imagine that such problems exist.

But if you are in any role where it's important for you to learn more about how to attract, promote, and retain great women in sales, I'm here to help. You will find resources in the book and online that can give you all that you need for success – if you are coachable and open to new ideas. If you do not have the support of your leadership, I can't promise much; but if you do, keep reading.

Before I share how you can attract more women to your open positions, let me tell you how to build a strong foundation for the changes you need to make to be successful.

CHAPTER TWO

Build a Foundation for Change

*"Learn from the mistakes of others. You can't live
long enough to make them all yourself."*

ELEANOR ROOSEVELT

In late 2020, I resumed swimming after many years. Quickly, I realized I'd forgotten my fundamental swim strokes, which hurt my ability to get a good workout at the neighborhood pool across the street. Swimming used to be my thing.

I could sign up to swim in advance since the Coronavirus outbreak limited access to a handful of people in the building at a time. Before getting back into the pool three times a week, I still wanted to be a better swimmer – it was a want. What could someone do to become a better swimmer?

- I could take lessons, but at the time, in-pool lessons were canceled
- I could watch YouTube videos and teach myself
- I could work on my strokes on land, and then when I get to the water, put them into action
- Or I could just wish and hope I'd be better

I employed each of these strategies with various results. Some worked, others didn't. I took action and didn't give up.

Building inclusive sales teams takes planning, it takes ideas, and putting new things in place. It takes real action – and sometimes switching up the action if what you're doing isn't working.

To improve my swim strokes, I tried new ways to learn and new things to do, and I didn't revert to my "old ways" of just thinking about it. I acted. When one video didn't help me, I tried another. When I felt little progress was being made, I had a video call with a swim instructor.

Like improving swim strokes, this book is about actually doing things to make a change and not just thinking or talking about it.

When I hear from an unhappy female seller, I work to understand the reasons. All too often, it is because of one of these:

- I feel like my company does not hear what I have to say
- I have been passed over for promotion in favor of male colleagues who are less deserving or less experienced
- I found out I have male peers making more than me for the same work
- My sales manager is a "bro," and what he says to me is hurting my mental health

Guess what 90% of these women do?

They move to another company where they feel they will be appreciated. In the current climate, you can't afford to lose great women in sales roles. In a February 2022 LinkedIn study of 20K+ workers in the U.S., 25% of Gen Z and 23% of Millennials said they hoped or planned to leave their current employer within the next six months. Rather than continue that trend we began, last year, calling the Great Resignation (or Great Reshuffle), isn't it really just time for new options and new ways to approach work?

I've adopted the mantra:
Go where you are celebrated, not tolerated.

It doesn't mean that it's a party every day at work. What it means is that salespeople on your sales team feel respected and heard. They know management appreciates them for who they are and what they bring. If they are female and strong in sales or sales management and are NOT feeling heard, they have options. I often, but not always, advise them: based on their situation, to "go." And they don't need me to tell them because retaining great women sellers and sales leaders can be difficult.

Diversity vs. Inclusion

Let's talk first about terminology. There is diversity, equity, inclusion (often grouped as DEI) Newer is the addition of "belonging" to DEI, or DEIB.

Many people use these terms interchangeably, but there is a huge difference between being told to include a candidate of color or a female candidate – and in thinking you have an inclusive sales team.

Diversity in sales could mean that someone has gone through the motions to include a range of candidates:

"We interview a woman in the mix as often as we can."

"We go to college job fairs and talk to as many diverse candidates as possible."

Diversity in sales could be that a non-majority candidate was hired.

Inclusion, on the other hand, is not only hiring a diverse group of employees but also welcoming and assimilating all new team members as part of the group. As someone who has been an "other" many times in B2B sales, it is the rare circumstance when a leader would ask me how they did, or how they are doing as it related to me feeling welcome and accepted. It is one thing to think you have a process that works and it is quite another to get feedback from those who are not in the majority.

New team members need onboarding that works for them, and a clear, documented ramp-up plan. Opinions and ideas are listened to, and leadership can show in multiple ways that they care about the entire team.

Here is some interesting data.

Research from the University of Colorado's Leeds School of Business:

Having more than one woman or minority candidate in the finalist pool would increase the likelihood of hiring a woman or minority beyond the increase you'd expect simply due to probability. The research found that when there were two female finalists, women had a significantly higher chance of being hired -79 times greater if there were at least two women in the finalist pool (controlling for the number of other men and women finalists).

Here are the five pieces of your foundation for success in moving from talk to action in creating a more inclusive sales culture:

1. It Starts at the Top

If TOP leadership is NOT involved and supportive, this initiative won't succeed. This is true with so many efforts within a company involving change, isn't it? Because change is hard, and it is easy to second guess a new process or goals or strategies without having a strong "why" and a champion for it at the top.

What does that look like?

It takes the form of "Who we are and what we stand for" visionary types of documents.

There is proof, not just words. Great proof can be as simple as posting photos on your website showing both male and female leadership. As women, we often expect the one-woman leader in HR or Marketing (or both). When we see a female president, CTO, CRO, or COO we take notice.

It's on your website and on third-party websites in the form of reviews and through referrals. We all look.

2. Create a Process and Make a Plan

You can't do everything overnight, but you can do something every day to improve. By creating an actual progress plan, you can track milestones and accomplishments and be reminded of who is overseeing each part of the initiative.

Here is an example of one activity that would go into the plan: Job Posting Makeover. You need to understand that many job postings have biased language in them. We discuss more about this in Chapter Three. Words like catalyst, fearless, quota crusher, warrior, sales savages, war room, and many other male-biased words need to be removed if you want more female applicants. There is a popular sales website today, as this book is going to print, where they refer to their members (sales professionals) as "savages." (Hint to the CEO, who is an acquaintance of mine: that term doesn't resonate with one half of the population.)

3. Follow the Data

I reference data throughout the book. It is compelling.

Gallup found that companies with more diversity have a 22% lower turnover rate, and if an organization has a more inclusive culture that embraces women, it's easier to recruit a more diverse staff.

More diversity leads to creative output from teams, which leads to better business. With more diverse team chemistry, you get new perspectives with more options to consider and more chances of having innovative solutions proposed.

There is also a lot of data about how many women have left the workforce during the COVID-19 Pandemic, and we need to find out how that has affected sales teams.

4. It takes Different Thinking to Create Results

Instead of doing the same things over and over and looking for a different result, try other ideas and see what happens. Since we lost so many businesses in the hospitality and service industries in 2020 and 2021, there are many great potential sellers who changed industries or are still wanting to. Either they landed somewhere temporarily, or they are still looking for the right role.

Find several new sources to look for a new stream of candidates. I offer some in the book as well as providing links to resources for updated lists of programs training non-majority candidates (including women) on SaaS sales fundamentals.

5. Understand What E.S.T. Is and Utilize It to Everyone's Benefit : Ethics, Safety, and Training

If your company has clear statements about the ethics that you follow, you will attract and retain more female candidates. If your company provides a sense of psychological safety and professional development, you will attract and retain more female (and all non-majority) employees. I have anecdotal data that will be backed up by research on this shortly.

When I talk about having clear statements, that's specifically what can best support you and demonstrate your company's values. Don't just talk about it. Put all of this in writing. Your mission, vision, and your "why" all need to be prominent for sales role applicants to see virtually and in person in the case of an office visit.

In the case of professional development (training): be clear. "We have 'X' dollars set aside annually for your development" or "We encourage internal candidates to be on a path to where they'd like to end up. To that end, we offer you the option to join one of 3 leadership development programs we've curated for you."

With a strong foundation in place, you will set yourself and your team up for an easier time with the changes that need to be thought about and implemented to improve your sales team. You can do it!

Next, I will show you how to attract great women to your sales team.

CHAPTER THREE

Attract Great Women to the Sales Profession

"All great achievements require time."

MAYA ANGELOU

Increasing the number of women in sales positions begins with attracting them to apply for sales positions. Build the pipeline. Maybe you've heard some evidence from an HP internal report that although men apply for jobs even when they are only 60% qualified, women don't typically apply unless they meet 100% of the stated qualifications. This discrepancy is typically explained by saying that women lack confidence.

Well, a research study published by the *Harvard Business Review* confirms the difference is true and sheds some new light on why.[6] Study author Tara Sophia Mohr was "skeptical" about the reason because she herself had chosen not to apply for jobs because she didn't meet all the qualifications, but it wasn't because she suffered from a lack of confidence. So, she conducted the study to investigate more deeply.

Mohr asked 1,000 men and women professionals: "If you decided not to apply for a job because you didn't meet all the qualifications, why didn't you apply?"

About 41% of women and 46% of men said: "I didn't think they would hire me since I didn't meet the qualifications, and I didn't want to waste my time and energy." This reason was more than twice as important as any other reason.

"What held them back from applying was not a mistaken perception about themselves, but a mistaken perception about the hiring process," Mohr concluded.

She believes women are more likely to be rule-followers than men and therefore are more likely to misunderstand that the ground rules for qualifications are often overturned when an otherwise great candidate shows up. So, it's not about a lack of confidence at all!

I wholeheartedly agree with both findings. In my experience, women don't want to waste time, theirs, or someone else's. If I don't have a serious shot at a position, why bother? It's a bad use of time for us both.

This finding suggests that how job descriptions are written is of great importance. If companies want to increase the number of women on their sales teams, they need to eliminate a laundry list of bullet points, include fewer "nice to haves," and instead focus on the basic requirements.

I have witnessed smart recruiting efforts that mention in the job description something like the following:

"If you don't meet every single qualification, please apply anyway. We encourage you in our effort for a more inclusive team."

Based on the research findings, the industry needs to re-think how to attract women to apply for sales positions.

If your company is not attracting female applicants for sales positions, you will not hire more women. Period. So, the place to start is to review the very beginning of your new-hire funnel.

Ask yourself these two questions:

- What are you doing to attract women applicants?
- Are you doing things unconsciously that deter women from applying?

I remember when fairly progressive male CEOs of startups would reach out and tell me that no women applied for sales roles, so how could they hire any? For a long time, that was the conventional thinking: just keep hiring the people who apply.

Eventually, I helped them evolve to where sales leaders and smart HR personnel started doing three things:

- Sourced unconventionally
- Changed the rules
- Removed bias thinking

These strategies changed the applicant pool for new hires in sales positions.

Source Creatively

Unconventional sourcing means looking for candidates in new places, places you traditionally haven't looked.

Instead of asking all of the sales reps (mostly male) if they could refer someone (more males) who might want a sales job, widen your net to look at places like college sales programs, hospitality, retail sales, and women in other internal positions within your own company (customer service or finance, for example) who would make good candidates for B2B sales roles. With the great lessening of SDR and BDR roles requiring college degrees, consider your own situation, and if a degree is not required, this opens up a much wider net for you to work with.

Post your job positions internally and circulate them. Hold an internal job fair for sales jobs. There are areas in your company, like human resources and marketing, where women outnumber men. Opportunities to advance and increase earning power are typically more limited in those areas than in sales. Why not make your case to those women?

Target your ads to reach women who are currently (or were previously) in retail sales and hospitality. A hospitality skill set can easily transition into successful B2B sellers, although I'd use an assessment tool to assess core sales competencies. Women who have worked in many retail or restaurant server positions could be your next SDR. I worked both retail sales and waitressed before I got my first tech sales role.

Top sales author of *"The Sales Development Playbook"* and my good friend Trish Bertuzzi was a server in a restaurant before one of her customers envisioned Trish's potential in inside sales and hired her for a sales role. The world of selling is fortunate that one visionary employer decided to take a chance on Trish. I've been grateful to have her as a colleague and mentor. Be creative in your targeting.

Hold virtual networking events to recruit new hires. The pandemic halted in-person events and gave us multiple opportunities to change what we thought of as standard and normal. We have learned how to host amazing virtual events that cast a wider net to a bigger potential group of candidates than ever before with a potentially worldwide audience. Use that to your advantage!

If you do hold an event virtually, change them to be more appealing to women as well as men. If you are hiring, host a "Virtual Lunch Hour" rather than an evening event. Send out Whole Foods gift cards for those located near them or a food delivery service to other attendees in the U.S. I am not sure of worldwide options for this other than using a virtual gift service for a similar effect.

When you hold an in-person event, be creative. Wistia, in Cambridge, MA, held a "Sales Bingo Night." They invited students, posted it socially, asked their sales team to invite people, and offered great prizes. They cobbled together a Bingo machine with the balls flying around inside of a container, had bingo cards and all the trappings, served appetizers, wine, and mocktails as well as beer, and held a great game night. Students and others employed elsewhere loved it and spread the word on social media about what a great place Wistia would be to work. Notice that in addition to finding a great candidate that night, the creativity and fun factor of the company spread socially, which is an important way to build a positive brand for future hires and for future customers.

This is different than holding another "panel about women in sales." As women, we are so done with that. Nearly every company has held one or sponsored one. It's time to think more creatively.

I spoke at the Peter T. Paul College of Business and Economics at the University of New Hampshire, where they have a sales minor. James McIlroy is the Director of the Sales Center. Once a year, they have a program to introduce women to the sales profession. The UNH Sales program and the Women in Business student group create an event that explains what sales is. They have a keynote and other speakers, plus a number of men and women from event sponsor companies. Students prepare questions in advance and break into small groups to interview guests in three rounds to meet three sets of different people. The event I spoke at was energizing and amazing. The sales team members from sponsor companies received visibility, which was good for them as sponsors.

Change the Rules

Changing the rules means eliminating or altering some hiring practices that became rules. One classic rule is when a sales leader (or CEO/president) insists that all sales candidates have a specific requirement, like an engineering degree or a computer science background for a technical sales role. In most cases, this requirement is not necessary! Sometimes it simply takes a new way of looking at roles on your team and whether there is role specialization. Someone who can pick up the phone, reach out by email, and socially begin conversations is one type of role specialization. I need no technical background to do that at your company. I've often challenged company leaders about this.

Without technical expertise around your products or services, I can come in and generate massive interest, and if there is a more technical person (or people) I can pull in or set up the next call with, it works extremely well. I'd suggest that it works better than your old way of one person doing many or all aspects of the sales process. I was never technically inclined, but I was a relationship seller, meaning that I could find the technical resource I needed to connect with my buyer to move a sales opportunity forward. Additionally, there are ways to gain the technical expertise necessary to succeed in technical sales if some are required, and that's why many have eliminated this nonsense rule in recent years.

Revamp your hiring requirements. If you have strict rules regarding requirements for credentials, degrees, years of experience, or particular kinds of experience, reconsider whether each requirement is really necessary for a salesperson to become successful or whether it is just a historical precedent. I can give you reasonable assurance that they aren't as necessary as you think.

Be aware of third-party posts about your company *(Glassdoor, Repvue, Blind* and *Bravado,* for example)* **and work to improve, if necessary.** If employees are reporting unpleasant practices in your company, take steps to address and change those practices. If you see a review that you believe to be unfair, you have the right to respond. You may also ask employees to post reviews about working at your company (without offering compensation or other perks in exchange for a good review.) Currently, it is a candidate's market with so many open positions. Your brand needs to be one that shows it is a good company to work for.

Remove the Biases That You Can

Bias-removal thinking means identifying all the barriers to entry for attracting more women, including women of color, to sales roles at your company. It encompasses every step of this process, from the actual job description, to what is said about your company on third-party sites, what the hiring process is like, and whether you incorporate recommendations that women candidates prefer.

First and foremost, everyone is biased in one way or another. The recent "awakening" of many in the majority population to systemic racism after the murder of George Floyd and others is helping create more diverse and inclusive leadership in the U.S. and hopefully elsewhere. It is hard work and involves difficult conversations. We still have a long way to go for the systems and general thinking to improve.

I had a difficult conversation with a male peer who thought that my feedback about a situation where he could have had more women involved was a personal attack. When people's defenses are up, we don't listen. We are not open to change. Creating conversation starters in your organization around all sorts of biases is a good regular activity to do. Getting people to talk openly is a strong first step.

Show transparency in hiring and promotions. Make the policies, procedures, and rules clear from the outset and communicate them clearly throughout your organization. There is no reason for secrecy; it only promotes distrust of management and "the system." Women need to believe that the system is fair and unbiased towards them. Everyone knows there has been bias in the past, if not in your company, then in other companies. Clarity and transparency will build trust. This is good for women, and it's good for everybody. Few benefit in a system that relies on favoritism or unspoken rules of engagement.

Re-write your job postings. Your job description is the first contact a woman may have with your company; Will it attract or repel her?

Hannah Fleishman, a recruitment marketer at HubSpot, wrote a post on the Hubspot.com blog called "Your Company's Job Descriptions are Driving Women Away."[7] She identified four themes in job descriptions that were potential problem areas in recruiting women:

- Qualifications: are they necessary? We know that women fail to apply unless they meet 100% of the stated qualifications. If you sometimes waive that requirement, state "preferred" or leave it out entirely
- Gender-related language: Certain phrases resonate more with men than women, such as "hacker" or "killer business instinct"
- Age-related perks: scooters and beer on tap are associated with youth
- "Company speak" language: phrases that don't make much sense to outsiders

From a broader perspective, create a clearer career path and paint a picture of the possibilities to attract women to apply for sales positions. Why not become a sales organization that is known for attracting and retaining women in sales positions and sales leadership?

We get a Re-do

The good news is that because of our shift to working remotely, the "male majority" focus of beer kegs and foosball in sales offices will never be the same again in much of Corporate America. As company offices opened back up, executive teams envision something bigger and different to get employees into the office at all. It's clear that there are and will continue to be fully remote workforces, and new ways are emerging to lure sellers back in together, at least periodically.

Now is the time to think about proximity bias: the idea that leadership treats those coming into the office differently than those remaining remote (or coming in less frequently). With women with families commonly working from a home office to retain precious commute time hours as time to get more done, they could be pushed away by leadership due to this bias.

Post on LinkedIn

One of my best tips to hire more diverse candidates has been for a VP of Sales, or another leader, to post on LinkedIn that they want to build an inclusive team and to please send candidates his (or her) way. You'll often see a list of great female SDRs, AEs, or sales leaders that one person will ask about, and everyone will comment on with their favorite person's name. Note those names, as they are people recognized for their work. It is a good beginning for a new connection. Everyone knows someone.

Search for #womeninsales on LinkedIn for other lists; I know of dozens.

Carolyn Murray started at DiscoverOrg (now ZoomInfo) as a Sales Development Rep and quickly became the company's first female Account Executive. Her blog post featured several ways to promote the sales profession to young women.[8] She starts with the first step of the Buyers' Journey: "Awareness." Three of Carolyn's recommendations:

1. Portray sales as a legitimate profession
2. Offer clear, specific encouragement
3. Re-evaluate your requirements

Carolyn's message comes down to this: We're in sales; we know how to sell something. If we want to sell our profession to women, try harder.

ZoomInfo is a leader and champion of inclusion. Years after Carolyn's promotion to AE, two different execs told me that Carolyn's promotion really got things going for them along the inclusion path. She has been incredibly successful. Zoominfo regularly supports groups and initiatives like events with Women Sales Pros.

Increasing the number of women on your sales team starts with attracting them in the first place. Your role in this can be as simple as improving your statement of job qualifications and revising position descriptions. It can be as broad as cultural change within your sales organization and the company at large. Or it can be as profound as influencing young women's perceptions of sales as a rewarding career and visions of themselves as sales professionals and sales leaders in the future.

I close this chapter with a story from Karianna Baretto, who was President of the UT Dallas Student Sales Board. Karianna wrote, "I competed in #utdsales Sales Pro Challenge for the second time and was the first student in UTD sales history to win the Cup twice. Our program has a saying that goes, 'Listen, Learn, Lead, leave a legacy.'[9] With the support and encouragement of students and faculty, I can now say I will leave a legacy."

Karianna completed a summer internship with IBM digital, participated in Outreach-sponsored events, and then landed a Microsoft summer internship. What will your sales organization have to offer to candidates like Karianna? How will you find them and attract them to apply?

TOP **10** TIPS

TO ATTRACT WOMEN

1. Re-think the hiring process

2. Look in unconventional places for talent

3. Review how you market your company

4. Create visibility for what's great there

5. Consider new faces to represent your company

6. Learn what employees who double as parents/caregivers want as benefits

7. Discover what others say about your sales team

8. Re-visit your job ads

9. Require a consistent hiring process.

10. Implement a pre-hire assessment tool for sales skills

CHAPTER FOUR

Hire Great Women for Your Sales Team

"You manage things; you lead people."

REAR ADMIRAL GRACE HOPPER

Now that you know how to attract more women to apply for your open sales positions, you need to rethink how you evaluate them for the job, understand how interviewing them is different from interviewing men, and you need to learn how to convince them to join your organization.

An important study in the *Harvard Business Review* titled "How We Describe Male and Female Job Applicants Differently"[10] found biases in letters of recommendation for women that raised doubts unrelated to quality or performance. The "doubt-raising" comments came from both women and men and were more frequently stated about female candidates.

The study defined doubt raisers as "short phrases that serve to (most often unintentionally) plant or raise some doubts in the minds of employers."

The three types they looked at were:

- Negativity: "She doesn't have much experience."
- Faint praise: "She needs only minimal supervision" *(but why should she need any supervision at all for this particular job?)*
- Hedges: "She might not be the best, but she will be good."

In a related study, this team found that references for women included more "communal words" like "sensitive," "caring," "kind," and "friendly" and that women even used such words more often in their resumes and letters of application.

In further studies, these authors found both the "doubt raisers" and the "communal words" had a negative impact on the people making hiring decisions about a pool of candidates.

The authors concluded that we need to counsel women and men about how they describe women in letters of recommendation to make sure they are not using "doubt raisers" and "communal words." We need to counsel women to avoid using "communal words" to describe themselves in job applications. They conclude, "Being fair means uncovering as many of the societal prejudices and biases that can pervade our selection systems."

What does this mean to you since you're not a counselor? Pay close attention to this kind of language when you read applications and references. Seek it out deliberately and see if you need to look past those words to the candidate's more meaningful credentials. Pass along this knowledge to others involved in hiring decisions.

Another HBR study concluded, "if there's only one woman in your candidate pool, there's statistically no chance she'll be hired."[11] In a series of controlled experiments looking at the odds of a female or racial minority candidate being chosen from an applicant pool of four candidates with the same credentials that in a pool of three men and one woman, the woman was never selected. However, in a pool of two women and two men, a woman was chosen 50% of the time.

The researchers suggest that people who are "the only one" in a pool of candidates are not hired because they differ from the "status quo." There is conscious or (more important) unconscious bias against hiring someone different. Having two women in the pool changes the status quo, giving the women a better chance of being chosen.

So, hiring managers wanting to increase the number of women in their sales organization and leaders who want to promote more women into sales leadership roles should work to get two or more women (or BIPOC) into contention for each available position.

As the research shows, hiring can be unintentionally biased against women in fields where women are a distinct minority, which they are in sales departments. So, if you really want to increase the mix of women on your sales team, you will need to do so deliberately.

Let's face it. The language of sales is male. If you think I exaggerate, here's a typical example. A post called "Traits of a Hunter: Finding Your Next 'Killer' Salesperson" calls out five qualities to look for when you are hiring.[12] Here are two of them:

1. Hunters have that natural 'fire in their belly.' When these people wake up each day, they rekindle a natural, innate drive to succeed. Their ambition to be the best drives their results and is ever-present. They tend to set very strong personal goals, have confidence in their abilities, and bring a high level of energy to their daily performance.

2. Hunters take control of the sales process. This is a critical trait for successful hunters because it is easy to get caught up in the prospect's process instead of their own. Taking control takes confidence, assertiveness, and a healthy amount of influence. Quality hunters set appropriate expectations and make sure they and the prospects are on the same page every step of the way.

Here's a list of words that are predominantly associated with males, as corroborated by this study by Pew.[13]

- **They are hunters**
- **Natural fire in their belly**
- **Natural innate drive to succeed**
- **Ambition**
- **Drive to results**
- **Very strong goals**
- **Confidence**
- **High level of energy**
- **Take control**
- **Assertiveness**

If your job descriptions include these phrases, or if leadership is speaking this way to the sales team, you may be relying on old-school, male-focused war words. This doesn't mean women are not competitive because many of us are. In my own case, I love to win, and I also don't like losing; however, I would not respond well to a job or career move where I would have to focus on competitiveness, as many former sales postings explained.

My list of "war-word" phrases that are real turn-offs to most women include:

- **Hunters who are hungry**
- **Sharks who are ready to go in for the kill**
- **Quota-CRUSHERS**
- **Sales warriors and soldiers**
- **Let's Kill It this quarter**
- **Let's Crush It**
- **Eat what you kill**
- **Bloody the water**
- **Killer instincts**
- **Assassin**
- **Killer**

Having 22 sales managers in my sales career, I found that many male sales leaders fall back on sports analogies as motivational tools. Sports analogies are fine some of the time, just not ALL of the time. You need to be aware that not everyone is a sports fan. Even I have made that mistake. Because I've spent decades in hockey arenas and love football, I have overloaded many of my conversations with sports analogies when describing business. A percentage of my audiences, men and women, have told me I included too many. Since everyone is not "all in" on the same things you or your leadership are, please remember to mix up the analogies, stories, and metaphors.

When sales execs want to hire sales reps with "killer instincts" and "sales animals" who perhaps were high school or college athletes, those descriptions don't always include smart, collaborative, innovative women. Top sales author and keynote speaker Jill Konrath said, "I was repeatedly told that I needed to 'play with the big boys' and to 'get in bed' with my customers. I learned that it was a 'war' out there, that my competitors were the enemy, and my job was to destroy them. [So] instead of focusing on products, services, and slimy sales techniques, I focused on my customer.

That's the only thing that mattered to me. I wanted to understand their status quo, their challenges, and their objectives."[14]

Against this background, which permeates our profession, making a hiring process gender-neutral and truly conducive to hiring women is a real challenge!

Revamping your hiring practices starts with your hiring philosophy and intentions.

Hiring Philosophy

You will need a high integrity, transparent, values-based approach to hiring. Be clear about your objectives. If you want to have more women in sales, let that be known to your team, throughout your company, and to outsiders. If you want a more inclusive sales team with more people of color, don't keep it a secret. Be clear about why it's important to you and how you are going about it. Give people opportunities to talk about your initiative, if that's what it is, and explain why it's important to sales and to your company more broadly. If some people want to gripe and complain, it's better to hear them out now than to allow them to sabotage your efforts during a hiring process or after a new woman is hired. I have way too many examples of that kind of behavior! As a leader, you need to guard against it.

Most people want to be fair, but when things are changing, it's easier to be fair when you have been made aware of that change, you have had a chance to be heard, you understand the rationale, and you know how it's going to happen.

I say a values-based approach because improving the mix of women and men in sales is a value decision. I'm providing you with a raft of reasons why that's a smart business decision that's good for sales and good for your company's bottom line. It's not a decision to be made grudgingly because someone said you have to.

It also ties in with my research on what women want to see in an employer, which I will discuss later in the book.

Ethical practices

Be sure you are up to date on legal and ethical hiring practices. Anyone who will be involved in interviewing candidates needs to know what constitutes discrimination, for example, especially in terms of illegal questions to ask women candidates. Just last week, a woman told me that a hiring VP asked her if she has children, so clearly, not everyone understands what to ask and what not to ask.

Cronyism, giving preferential treatment to someone that you know or is known to a member of your team, is another unethical practice. It's very common in sales and works against women and people of color since they are in such a minority in this industry.

Be very clear about the requirements of the position, and don't change them after someone is hired.

"Culture Fit"

A lot has been said and written about how the practice of hiring for "culture fit" has been responsible for keeping women and minorities out of much of the sales community. I've talked to countless women who define sales as a "bro" culture in which they don't fit and where they are not welcome. That's only one descriptor, but it's rampant. If this is the culture of your sales group and you are hiring for culture fit, it's obvious that women are not going to be selected. It's equally obvious that even if you demand that a woman or two be hired, they are unlikely to be successful in that cultural environment.

What works better is to hire people who align with your professional core values or mission rather than culture. If you don't have a clear set of value statements for the sales team, now is a good time to work with people to develop them. Get multiple people involved. Invite women from other areas of the company to help if you don't have women on your team to be sure that your value statements aren't inadvertently biased towards male values. It's better to state values as a sentence rather than a single word to be more inclusive.

For example, "strong" is a value more often associated with men than with women. But the value statement "We are strong supporters of our colleagues and promote each other's success" applies equally to women and men. If your culture is rife with the language in my opening volley, it probably needs some attention to be inclusive. It's not that many women don't have the traits of a "killer" instinct or a natural, innate drive to succeed. It's just that a preponderance of male-dominant language makes her feel excluded. You can make the same point with some simple changes.

If your team needs help, ask them what their clients want to see in a salesperson. Do they want a "killer" who "takes control of their process?" Or do they want a different kind of relationship? Putting customers in the center helps to temper the language decisions!

During your interview process, share a vision for what the opportunity could entail and how someone could learn and develop in the role. Show through transparency that salaries are the same for people at the same levels. Describe what an actual sales career progression could look like. Explain benefits that go beyond those of parents. Not all women are mothers or want to be! Opportunity and professional development are important to women and will help them decide to come on board with you if a position is offered. If she will be the first woman on a team of men or one of a very few, you will have a sales job to do in order to hire the woman candidate of your choice.

Assessment

Use a third party validated sales pre-hire candidate assessment tool, so you don't become enamored with the wrong candidates. Hunches have always been trouble for sales leadership. I know that when I was a sales manager, I never was better than 50% right in terms of hiring the right reps for my team. Somehow, we feel like we're good at it the longer we're around or, the more we've seen. Hiring the right salespeople or knowing where you're at without analyzing sales datasales data is just not possible. I'm a huge fan of data in any way, shape, or form I can get it.

It's easy to get excited about people during the interview process. You just like them! Everyone can see them as a colleague. But likability is only one of many qualities that you need in a new member of your team. It often depends on how much that person "fits in" or seems like the others. It can reveal unconscious bias and work against hiring women. That's why using a standard assessment at an early stage of your hiring process can guard against this kind of mistake. An assessment tool can keep you from falling in love with any one candidate.

Your hiring managers need to understand the differences between men and women candidates. For example, there are many studies that show women are not typically strong at self-promotion. Women tend to downplay their accomplishments. You can see how this could skew more toward male candidates when interviewing male and female reps or leaders.

What can a hiring manager do?

Ask more questions to better understand what a candidate has accomplished rather than skip over it.

Create a fair process

What's most important is to be sure your process is fair and work to make it that way. A few key checkpoints include:

- Have a streamlined, consistent hiring process. Make the rules simple, clear, and transparent
- Ask the same questions of every candidate
- Have women from the company involved in the hiring process, not just men, even if your team is all male. This practice will help counter bias or unconscious bias of "like hires like" and "culture fit"

When you have a new *(or improved)* hiring process in place, you'll be ready to bring some new women on board. As you will learn in Chapter 5, there are differences in the way you should onboard women to help retain them.

TOP **10** TIPS

TO HIRE MORE WOMEN

1. Watch the words you choose

2. Have a consistent, solid hiring process that everyone follows

3. Reduce your "nice to haves" in the job description

4. Improve your job posts overall

5. Reduce male-focused words in job descriptions

6. Use fewer bullet points when describing a role

7. Have female sales team members or leaders involved in the interview process

8. Offer the same compensation for similar work

9. Keep your hiring process moving, so candidates don't wait too long

10. Use a transparent, values-focused hiring process

CHAPTER FIVE

Onboard Great Women Successfully

*"The most common way people give up their pow-
er is by thinking they don't have any."*

ALICE WALKER

Great. You've hired several women to join your team. Rather than treating them as "one of the guys" (pardon my inconsistent grammar for emphasis on the phrase), you now need to onboard them successfully so they will stay.

Onboarding both men and women is an important process that many companies ignore. Just a couple of years ago, Gallup found that only 12% of employees strongly agreed that their organization does a great job of onboarding. Given today's remote work imperative, I wonder what the new number would be.

Do you have a formal onboarding process? Does it take into account the different values women bring to the position? One of the first things you need to understand is that women think differently about work than men. Women value the organizational support they receive, career clarity, and the training and coaching offered to them.

Therefore, you should address those aspects as part of the onboarding process. When bringing new women into a sales department, you should consider including:

- Visible support from your organization
- An introduction to the career path or paths available to salespeople
- An exemplary onboarding program that includes future training opportunities throughout her career in your sales department

Once you have hired some new sales reps, your most important job is to bring them on board in a way that makes them feel welcome, glad that they've joined your company, excited about their new job, and looking forward to the time ahead.

Let's start with some ideas about onboarding in general, not only about sales. UrbanBound, a relocation management software company, posted an infographic with statistics about relationships between a company's onboarding program and the future success of its new hires. Here are some important points about onboarding programs, not limited to sales:

- 20% of turnover occurs within the first 45 days of employment
- Organizations with a standard onboarding process experience 54% greater new hire productivity
- Employees of companies with the longest onboarding programs gain full proficiency 34% faster than those in the shortest programs
- 77% of new hires who hit their first professional milestone had formal onboarding training
- 70% of employees say having friends at work is the most crucial element to a happy working life

Talmundo, a company that provides onboarding software to help HR teams manage the onboarding process for their new hires, offers specific suggestions for bringing women on board.[26]

They mention that many businesses have a recorded message from the CEO. But given that your CEO or founders are likely males, you could also have a video from a female leader or leaders to welcome your new female hires, especially if they are not many women in their role at the company.

When they are in the minority, women may find it harder to feel comfortable and that they are bringing their whole selves to work. This ultimately means they might become less engaged, less productive, and, worst-case, leave altogether. Talmundo suggests, and Dr. Le Bon and my research confirm, that you can help new women reps and leaders by building-in networking and socializing opportunities from day one. Do this across the business, not just in sales. Talmundo reports, "People with a best friend at work are seven times more likely to be engaged."

Be Proactive

Best practice employee onboarding means checking in with all employees actively. Pay attention to things like whether women are being assertive with other team members. Are their voices being heard in meetings? Are the new women attending virtual (and eventually, in-person) social events that you have planned? Do they volunteer for extra responsibilities? These are all signs that they feel they are fitting in. You need to seek feedback regularly from new hires. Not just randomly but deliberately.

Every rep, no matter how senior they are, when they come into a new sales environment, needs to be trained on your company's sales process, mindset, and goals to make sure that everyone is aligned. It's a myth that more senior salespeople can just be left alone to do their thing because it doesn't work that way. We need to interact, coach, mentor, and help inspire every sales rep. Particularly the newer ones.

One Women Sales Pros client, a multi-billion-dollar company in the building trades, has a 90-10% split between men and women on the sales team. What is tough here is that sales is a male-majority role and the building trade is a male-majority industry. The company typically onboarded all new reps at corporate, and then reps would go off to their assigned geographic territory. When a new rep was female, she would start in her geographic territory as the only woman (or one of a couple in much bigger groups of male reps and leaders). What we learned when we brought all of the women together for their first Women in Sales offsite was that they longed to meet women in other geographic territories to learn more from them, which they believed would allow them to ramp up more quickly.

One result of our offsite was a new policy: now, a new woman seller can put in a request to travel and "ride along" with a woman in another territory, which is highly encouraged and supported.

It takes a very strong onboarding program for male and female reps to thrive in their sales role. This means more "just-in-time" doses of learning and reminding on an ongoing basis rather than a data dump for three days or two weeks and then "see you later." It doesn't work that way. Adults learn through repetition and reinforcement. Many of us in the training business (and those of you buying sales training) know about the Ebbinghaus Forgetting Curve - information is lost in a matter of days or weeks unless a strong reinforcement program with interactivity is in place. Otherwise, new reps lose about everything covered in onboarding, other than key points.

Put the Buyer First

Most of the time spent in sales training is product training. Understanding the features and advantages our products and services have is important; however, today, new reps need to learn about your buyers first. How do you help different companies and different industries? One way to address this during onboarding is to share any recordings you may have of top reps talking to customers so the new reps can get a feel for their new world. Then they can learn all about what you're selling. Feature-based selling is old school and will show your new reps a lack of relevance for today's buyers (and sellers).

I helped onboard over 1,000 reps in a 3½ year period not too long ago. What new reps say they want to know is, "What do I do? Just tell me what to do. I'll do it." That's like telling you to paint a beautiful painting and expecting it to come out incredible. You need to first learn some basic paint types, painting brushes, and the strokes they create. And to understand some basic design principles like perspective. Then you can move into something more challenging and advanced. Most people understand that there's an art to sales. It's not just all science and data.

A person should come into a new sales role as an apprentice. If they are open to learning and ideas, they can adapt with their own personality and put a little twist on it in terms of how they communicate with people. That's what makes selling an amazing profession. It really is a craft.

Whenever I hear people talk about women who are very successful sales-people, they typically highlight that women are exceptionally good at connecting with buyers. If that is a special talent that women offer, all the more reason to make it prominent in your onboarding program. That practice will be good for all your new hires.

Go Beyond

Onboarding needs to cover more than the sales knowledge and product knowledge that your new reps will need. When I looked online for sales onboarding advice, I found dozens, if not hundreds, of formulas for 30-, 60-, and 90-day programs. While a few included information about the company and its mission and values, most covered only various skills and techniques associated with selling and learning about the product. But what I learned from the research is that women have different expectations from men about what is important to their job satisfaction and commitment to a sales career, and these feelings develop very early in a new position.

Women, generally more than men, want to see the ethics of their new company they have come into demonstrated and also what kind of support their department has from senior leadership for professional development. Our research shows that feeling welcome and a part of the team is critical. New reps will expect their onboarding process to make opportunities available for socializing in an environment where they feel comfortable and included. Women, more than men, want to know what kind of career path this position will provide. These areas should be part of your onboarding plan.

Vary Learning Styles

People have very different learning styles and preferences. Many people believe that women have some learning style differences from men, but I am not sure I can confirm that. It's clearly true that people differ in how they learn. So, your onboarding program should always include multiple forms of presentation, including working with text materials, listening and discussing, watching and observing, and hands-on doing and being immersed in practice. If you introduce multiple ways for people to learn new material, more of them will learn, and more of their learning will remain with them over time.

Your sales managers play a significant role in a new hire's onboarding experience. If they have been promoted to a management position from a sales role, they will need training to participate appropriately in the onboarding program and to support new hires, especially women who are coming into a male-majority environment. The best onboarding program on earth will fail if your sales managers are unequal to their job.

Virtual Onboarding Considerations

In a time of virtual onboarding, it is even more critical to get onboarding right from the beginning. Even when in person, onboarding can be a challenge. When I started at Fintech company CCBN as employee #35, the president had begun taking new sales hires to lunch on the day they started. He did that because previously, someone had worked the very first day until noon, left for lunch, and never returned. Obviously, this person's first impression was that this company wasn't for her or him. It was so bad that the person didn't even care to address it with upper management. What better way to have a first impression than lunch (in-person or virtual) with the president or CEO? Of course, lunch with the C-level execs may not be scalable. However, the story is a good reminder of the importance of first impressions.

Virtual onboarding can be tough without a well-thought-out plan that sticks with the vision and goals of your organization. In advance, your hiring manager(s) and execs need to be clear on how they will communicate the company's way of working, understand the best practices in remote learning, and convey empathy for each new person's situation and environment. Mailing a "pre-boarding" physical package is a very nice touch, and sending a simple survey at the end of each day during onboarding can show the new reps your level of interest, especially if any issues are brought up and addressed. These are just a couple of initial ideas within a very big topic.

2023 brings more in-person initial training or at least quarterly/semi-annual sales reviews and annual kickoffs.

Take Small Steps to Bolster Onboarding Programs

I've suggested a number of things that may be add-ons to your current onboarding program, and maybe you're worried about how to fit it all in. It's not too hard if you think differently. You don't have to finish the onboarding program before people start to work!

Look at it as basic training followed by six months or more of coaching and extended support. Continue to offer opportunities for dialogue, networking, social events, brown bag lunches, speakers, or career presentations as long as it takes to properly socialize all your new hires into your sales culture.

Work with your HR department as you redesign your onboarding program. Strike a balance between sales content and other content best-suited to make new hires, especially women, have an exceptional experience with your company during their earliest weeks and months.

Congratulations! You've successfully onboarded several women to your sales team. But your work isn't over. Now you need to learn what you need to do to make them stay, which I address in the next chapter. Hint: it starts with your sales managers.

TOP **10** TIPS

TO ONBOARD WOMEN

1. Understand your new hires have style differences and respect those

2. Teach your sales managers about style differences and regularly coach your managers

3. Share company values and professional development opportunities

4. Have a mentor program to support all on your team

5. Implement policies for parental leave for sales (commission on reps' deals closed while gone, as well as better ramp up upon return than standard)

6. Ensure you have a solid, formal program for new hires that focuses on who your buyers are and how you serve them. Get outside opinions from sales experts and/or educators

7. Introduce new sales hires to executives in other areas of the company.

8. Have leadership discuss how sponsors in the company can impact career growth

9. Create an effective, formal coaching program for once-a-week coaching or more

10. Solicit input from the new hires on what is important to them and how their onboarding is going. Upon completion, ask for feedback on ways to improve for future new hires

CHAPTER SIX

Retain Great Women
for Continued Success

"Trust is like glass – once broken, it will never be the same again."

AUTHOR UNKNOWN

Once any SDR, BDR, AE, or other rep –male or female –becomes a part of the sales team, the new focus is on their successful professional development, promotion, and ultimate retention.

I have found over the years that there are great sales teams, and there are not-so-great sales teams. Leadership is the difference. Great teams are led by individuals who have a servant-leader mindset who appreciate those on the team and coach each team member in a personalized way to enhance their strengths and help build where they are less strong.

Before you can retain the women you hire, you need to make sure you have strong managers and leaders who understand that managing women is different and make sure they understand their role in retention.

Provide Strong Leaders

As my research shows, women's job satisfaction is highly associated with supportive leadership. And as the Gallup research shows, business, in general, is not doing well at providing great leaders. In sales, the problem is even more severe for several reasons.

First, sales managers are "overwhelmed and underdeveloped," as the title states in the CSO Insights 2017 report on Sales Manager Enablement.[15] The report points out that while formal enablement efforts to improve the effectiveness of sales managers had increased for the last several years, sales quota attainment continually decreased during the same time period.

In a time of pandemic or even the recovery and "next phase" of business, the uncertainty and change, not to mention grief and fear for some, have added additional overwhelm.

The B2B sales tradition still tends to promote sales reps into sales managers. But it's a position that's not at all like the position they've occupied before, often with a misunderstanding as to whether their skills and competencies are a good fit. For this reason, CSO Insights suggests that "Bad habits formed early on or adopted by emulating their managers become engrained and are repeated year after year, with much the same results. They develop an unconscious competence, but one that exhibits all of the wrong behaviors. Worse, when sales get stressful, these bad habits are magnified."

Second, it's true that both men and women new hires have the same sales managers. But I've learned that supportive leadership is much more important to women in terms of job satisfaction.

Fewer sales managers are women. Typically, it is easier for male sales managers to relate to the men they manage than to the women. I've often seen that strong thread of sports discussion happening in sales conversations as one way a manager endears himself with his team. Perhaps it is because the sales manager is a huge sports fan. We know that sports connect men in a way that society has reinforced for more than 150 years. As the lone woman or one of a few women on a sales team where sports is incessantly discussed, it can be irritating at best and enough for some women to choose to work elsewhere.

We can't generalize by gender, and I'm not trying to. I am an ice hockey fan, and I love to talk about pro and collegiate hockey. I was and will always be a hockey mom. I went a little crazy during the pandemic when sports stopped and continued to be shut down. Most women don't want to hear me go on and on about hockey or most other sports. Some men don't, either.

In my case, I "joined" the sports discussion over the years by learning more about baseball, golf, football, and hockey. I was conversational and appreciative of the main storylines and characters for each sport every season. What I came to learn as a sales manager myself was that if others don't all relate to your stories and analogies, you need to have alternative ones and mix your stories up. In sales team meetings, don't go on and on about any one topic – especially sports.

This leads me to mention that if a female rep on a male-majority sales team doesn't feel respected or feels that she is not taken seriously regardless of the topic, it's important she should be heard. When a woman in sales comes to us with this situation (more often than you might think), we encourage her to talk about it with her supervisor. If her supervisor is part of the problem, which is very often the case, she needs to know how to resolve the issue without making her situation worse.

Third, research has proven that recognition motivated women to stay in their roles. For the early stages of a rep's career, that recognition is most likely to come from her sales manager or within the manager's team of reps. If the manager is not skilled at providing appropriate recognition when the job is done well, women tend not to stay.

Finally, leadership is critical because of culture. If your sales area has a toxic bro culture, few women will stay, and those who do will have a very difficult time. Even if you have a more neutral culture, if it is exclusively male, introducing one or two women will change the dynamics significantly.

Leaders need to set the tone. Any failure in creating a more inclusive sales team stems from the top of the company in the C-suite and other leadership, such as investors and advisors. If you have four male co-founders and your first HR hire is not empowered to bring up gender bias issues, that's on you. If you are CEO at a mid-market company and pre-pandemic knew of sales managers who used to take their team to a bar for meetings, that's on you. Leadership sets the tone. Biases, whether implicit or explicit, have been around forever in how we were all raised and how we were socialized, starting as kids. It doesn't disappear just because a smart sales leader wants a diverse sales team.

Improving the retention of the women you hire will absolutely require getting sales managers on board with the plan and providing training to help them become better leaders, not just on the sales side but on the people side.

We know that training managers to be effective coaches improves their performance and the performance of their teams, regardless of gender. That's one place to start. Offer training on unconscious gender bias for your entire sales team, women and men alike. Everyone has biases. Be sensible when assigning new women recruits to a sales manager. Don't assign her to a man who has expressed negative ideas about "diversity hires." On the other hand, don't assign all the women to a female sales manager. You may be thinking that I am not aware it is 2023. I am. Someone just relayed a story to me about a male manager who didn't want women on his team.

You can't change it all overnight, but you can make smart choices along the way.

Go for Inclusion, not Diversity

Understand the differences between diversity and inclusion. Diversity means you made the hires. You hired women into a mostly male team or people of color into a mostly white team. Forcing diversity into an organization will not have any positive effects unless the culture is welcoming to the people who differ from the majority. It is not your opinion, as the majority, if they are feeling welcomed, valued and appreciated but rather it is their opinion.

McKinsey & Company reports that while 90 percent of companies say they prioritize gender diversity, only 42 percent of employees think that is the case. That perception comes from the difference between diversity or hiring women, and inclusion, which is making a diverse organization the norm where everyone is welcome.

The real goal is inclusion, and in the context of this book, it means that sales not only hires women but welcomes them in tangible ways to the team. This includes BIWOC (Black, Indigenous, and women of color). Inclusion means we all work together, are valued for our opinions, and offer our buyers diversity of thought.

Just as I suggested lots of differences in how you attract women to your sales team; I recommend you pay attention to the kinds of things you do as a team to have fun, let off steam, and celebrate. This extends to both formal and informal events, both in and out of the office, virtually, or on the road at trade shows or client visits.

If there's a preference for drinking, nightclubs that cater to men, or other venues where women would feel unwelcome or uncomfortable, just stop doing that. Don't sponsor events that are not equally appropriate for women and men. When you do active sports, be certain that women are encouraged to participate, not just tolerated. Invite some women from other departments to change up the balance or do more joint events with other departments in general, just to improve alignment. In the "new work world" where most of us are remote and getting together less often, it really matters when we do get together that it is a positive environment for all.

This was one of those bright spots during 2020 and much of 2021. No events or extracurricular activities happened in person; therefore, nothing could be deemed inappropriate. Everyone has had to learn how to relate to all in the group in virtual ways. Going forward, it will be interesting to see how much of a hybrid model we'll have for in-person versus remote events.

There are still male-majority industries where hunting, fishing, and golf are regular sales rep/channel rep/client activities. Clearly, these are activities that many women may not care to participate in. However, as with anything else, rather than continue age-old traditions and what you've always done, think more inclusively and offer different options.

I have never been asked to go on a fishing or hunting weekend with clients. But I have been invited to dinner in dark steak houses and post-dinner cigars in cigar bars. Men, you don't have to give this up; you just need to think and get input from others about what everyone thinks is a fun time, not just the same people who have always decided in the past.

I never went to a strip club for a meeting, but I was invited to attend. This is where we draw the line and remind you as leaders that you're running a professional business and use professionalism as your guide when thinking up events and activities.

Also, don't assume that because someone is a woman, she won't be interested in a particular event or outing. Don't assume because someone is a single parent; they won't be interested. I was excluded from some after-work events because my colleagues knew I was a single parent. I wasn't even invited. No one wants you to decide for them. My teammates would have been MUCH better off having invited me, with me politely passing if I didn't have a way to get childcare (or if I didn't want to attend).

A woman sales leader recently told me how disappointed she was that her own sales reps went over her head to her male boss to invite HIM to a sporting event with their prospects. Her boss went, and no one told her until after the event. I would have been fuming if that was me.

Do you have team sales for key accounts or bigger deals? Those are great places to start diversifying your sales operation. A more diverse team will not only bring people together with a common purpose but will out-perform an all-male or all-female team. Success breaks down barriers fast. Any kind of sales team activity is important in building a culture of inclusion.

Fix Problems

Women on mostly male sales teams still face considerable problems in the workplace, some more serious than others, but all demoralize, deflate, and affect retention. Time and time again, I've learned that it is not one big thing that has happened, but many little things (known as microaggression) and certainly the feeling that one is being passed over for promotion or other opportunities.

Here are a few of the things you can do to retain the women sellers you want to keep:

- Use an assessment tool to evaluate existing sales team members in an objective way. Train all managers on how to use it and how often. This will work to eliminate bias in performance evaluations

- Help reps set goals and create plans to attain their goals. Review regularly

- Coach all reps—even the seasoned, tenured reps

- Ensure front-line managers are coached and trained on the diversity of thought and that most women accomplish sales differently than most men

- Value and listen to all team members. Not being heard is a primary reason women leave. Pay attention to how women's ideas are received in meetings and whether they can speak without interruption

- Create a flexible workplace, one where a parent, male or female, can work and succeed. Many women in sales report demotions and other loss of opportunities while they are pregnant or upon returning from maternity leave. If a rep takes maternity leave, how is her book of business handled? Is she given a split on her deals that someone else closed while she was gone, and can she ramp up to full productivity once she returns? Departments other than sales are doing much better in providing flexibility for parents, especially during pregnancy and soon after the birth of a child

- Be sure that quotas, territories, compensation, and opportunities are determined objectively, with clear and transparent criteria. There is clear evidence that women have sometimes been given inferior territories in hopes they would fail. They discover that their quotas are higher than the men's. Or that their compensation packages have been inferior to their male counterparts for years. Check this out in your area, and if necessary, correct it

Executive leaders who share and post very clear company values, like "We respect everyone here," offer support to a rep or front-line leader who is not feeling appreciated. Someone on this company's sales team who doesn't feel respected can cite the company values and look to a mentor or sponsor in the company when the immediate supervisor is not helping.

Ultimately, a company cannot afford to pay women on their sales teams less than their male counterparts or treat them any less respectfully. There are too many companies just waiting for one of your top reps to share some of their displeasure with their role, and the floodgates of opportunity will open.

If your company leadership is not fully bought into solving sales team issues, they won't get fixed. I worked with a manufacturing company where the VP of Sales wanted to know everything there was to know about his sales team. He wanted to pull data apart and get feedback on his reps and his leadership and their process and pipeline. I helped them put new ideas and systems in place, but ultimately the CEO of the company did not support it. Even with the best of intentions in mid-level or senior mid-level management, it wasn't enough to override the fact that at the very top, there was a leader who only wanted to do what they used to do. Because that's what he was comfortable doing.

Change is tough. When you're working to improve your sales team, you have to make changes, and those changes have a ripple effect. You need to embrace that, and your leadership needs to be behind things 100%

from the top down to do so successfully.

Retaining women requires more than being welcoming. Promoting women into leadership roles is also critical, and I'll share several tips to help you do that in the next chapter.

TOP **10** TIPS
TO RETAIN WOMEN

1. Use your formal coaching program to coach all who want coaching, not just reps in the middle or just newer reps. BDRs, SDRs, and AEs should be coached weekly

2. Explain to women reps the options for their career path as a seller, in enablement, or customer success. Are there other paths to explore?

3. Offer regular feedback instead of quarterly or less

4. Pay your female reps and leaders the same way you pay your male reps and leaders!

5. Don't be afraid to highlight successes publicly on LinkedIn and elsewhere

6. Use a formal process for promotion into sales leadership

7. Be clear about how one can rise within the organization

8. Support #WomenInSales efforts outside of your organization

9. Create or offer support for an internal women in sales group/community

10. Ask for feedback from your women sellers as to whether they have suggestions to make your environment more welcoming

CHAPTER SEVEN

Promote Great Women

*"Life is like riding a bicycle.
To keep your balance, you must keep moving."*

ALBERT EINSTEIN

Throughout the past few decades, you've probably heard a lot of people discuss a 'glass ceiling' that prevents women from reaching senior leadership positions. "In reality, the biggest obstacle that women face is much earlier in the pipeline, at the first step up to manager. Fixing this broken rung is key to achieving parity." So says the Women in the Workplace 2019 study by McKinsey & Company[16] and Sheryl Sandberg's Lean In organization.[17]

For every 100 men promoted and hired to manager, only 72 women are promoted and hired. This "broken rung" results in more women getting stuck at the entry-level and fewer women becoming managers. Not surprisingly, men end up holding 62 percent of manager-level positions, while women hold just 38 percent.

Although representation of women in senior management has improved since 2015, there's still a long way to go. In the 2022 LeanIn "Women in the Workforce" study, women represented 48% of all employees at the entry-level, but here's how the percentages shrunk at every level of promotion:

Women in The Workplace: Key Findings 2022

	ENTRY LEVEL	MANAGER	SR. MANAGER/ DIRECTOR	VICE PRESIDENT	SENIOR VICE PRESIDENT	C-SUITE EXECUTIVE
WHITE MEN	33%	41%	47%	54%	58%	61%
MEN OF COLOR	19%	19%	16%	14%	13%	13%
WHITE WOMEN	29%	27%	26%	24%	23%	21%
WOMEN OF COLOR	19%	14%	10%	8%	6%	5%
TOTAL WOMEN IN 2022	48%	40%	36%	32%	28%	26%
TOTAL WOMEN IN 2017	47%	37%	33%	29%	21%	20%
% POINT CHANGE FROM 2017	+1%	+3%	+3%	+3%	+7%	+9%

Source: https://leanin.org/women-in-the-workplace

We know that women don't represent even close to 48% of entry-level positions in sales, so the percentages of women in sales management shrink even further at every level of leadership, with more like 12-15% women in C-level executive sales roles.

The study also acknowledges that senior leadership and leadership at the management level are both critically important in order to fix this broken rung. It found very positive change among senior leaders, both men, and women, in their active commitment to improving gender diversity in their companies. However, among people who are managers, while 53% of men say "gender diversity is a priority," and 64% of men "have participated in unconscious bias training," only 13% of men are "actively working to address diversity and inclusion."[18] That's a terribly low number of male managers really working at removing barriers to women's success.

This statistic suggests that sales organizations have a lot of work to do before sales managers are actively seeking to promote the women sales reps in their charge.

While studies have shown there are many reasons women aren't promoted, I believe there are three main reasons:

- Societal issues
- Company or sales culture
- Women ourselves

Societal Issues

Throughout society, there exists an unconscious bias: men lead, and women support or are caregivers. This thought permeates much of the underlying system that holds women back in business. While some men (and women) may disagree, I remind you that we're talking about unconscious, not intentional or conscious bias. Without spending too much time on this, I will share a fantastic resource at the end of the book that can help intentional people combat gender bias in the workplace.

Two items need to be discussed when we speak of societal issues. The first is that women are still considered primary caregivers in most North American homes. When the pandemic hit and schools shut down, it was often the women with children who bore the brunt of an attempt at "homeschooling" plus their job in a new "work from home" way. Kudos to the men who DO half of the work at home. I know some of you and appreciate you so much. Single moms with kids and those women doing most of the homemaking have had to make tough decisions. One woman I know said that she could not keep up with her kids' schedules and hit her sales quota (which initially did not get reduced), so she switched to a customer care role. Faced with this decision, I wondered what others would do. Statistics recently shared by Outreach's Mary Shea showed that we may have lost 10% of the women who were in B2B sales roles since 2020.

I would be remiss at this time not to address the massive disparity in our amazing B2B sales world around the lack of people of color, now often referred to as BIPOC. As a privileged white woman, I used to think I should just stick to what I knew as a woman and not speak about racial and ethnic inclusion. I have a platform and I have a voice, so I will speak up. You will not see me in a current virtual or live event speaking about more women in sales without me also speaking about people of color, especially my Black and Brown sisters in sales or those who want to get INTO sales. I'm energized by the discussions and efforts going on for more social justice. I hope the efforts do not stop, and I will do my part to not just speak but continue to act.

Company/Sales Culture

One of the issues that continues to be appalling is the mentality among some men that women won't last long in sales positions because of the future possibility of their having children. And while you may dismiss this notion as historical, statements to this end are still happening.

On multiple occasions at our "Rising Stars" event for women newer to sales, we were told by a number of women that they didn't think they could ever leave to have a child and come back – and keep their sales role.

What?
Heads nodded. Women commiserated with each other. How could they rise in sales and have a family? I heard this comment at two different events a year apart.

With this in the backs of the minds of some of your fantastic hires, you need to have a strong, supportive, and clear family policy in place. If you are a startup, consider your parental leave policy as an important early piece of content to have for your employees. Don't wait until they come to you about it because the minute someone mentions "family leave," we know that people immediately think they are asking for a reason, and that person is not treated the same afterward.

And let me be clear here: sales roles that have a percentage of OTE as commission and/or bonuses need family leave policies that take into account payment of commission or bonus when on leave if a deal the rep or manager was to receive compensation for as well as a ramp up a policy where one is not at "zero" when returning.

Women Themselves

Societally, women don't generally seem to have the same need to want to be #1 or have a statue created in their image. The same is true about promotion. Because of how we were generally raised and socialized, women are not knocking down the door of leadership about promotions. You may need to make a compelling case for a woman on your team to grow in the leadership ranks.

Women don't always raise their hands for a promotion because they don't think you (the leader) will notice our work and efforts. By tapping a woman rep on the shoulder and letting her know you see her potential, you'll solve that. By helping her or encouraging her to create a promotion plan, you'll be proactive. The other issue is that a good percentage of women like being individual contributors (I know I certainly did) because we control our destiny, our income, and our efforts.

So, it is not one simple thing. It is a combination.

Study this chapter forward and backward because it is the key to your inclusive sales team.

How to Fix the Broken Rung

"The broken rung" is much more serious than "the glass ceiling" in the sales arena. In business, this is the first promotion to manager, and anecdotally, I believe that in sales, it may be that next promotion from sales manager to whatever that next step is in your sales organization – often a Sales Director role. How can you fix the broken rung in your sales department and, ultimately, in your company?

Have a fair and transparent process for promotion

Especially where women are concerned, understanding the career path is an important item when desiring to stay with their company. In *The Sales Development Playbook*, Trish Bertuzzi reports that sales managers expect a rep to stay in a position 21 months before promotion, but the reps expected a promotion after 15 months.[19] That kind of disconnect damages relationships and retention. Trish recommends a path of "micro-promotions" for SDRs. For example, "hire in as a junior SDR, promote to associate SDR, and then elevate to senior SDR." This allows for career path movement prior to the time when promotion to Account Executive is likely to occur. These micro-promotions, of course, need to have achievement requirements attached, and the path to achievement should be clearly articulated during the hiring process and onboarding.

Lately we have noticed after just one year a BDR often wants to move into an AE role even though the two roles are very different and success is uncertain.

Making the process for promotion "fair" is not easy. A 2018 study reported by McKinsey argued that three factors contribute to creating a process that employees find "fair":

- Link goals to business priorities
- Invest in managers' coaching skills
- Reward outstanding performance and manage converging performance[20]

Linking goals to business priorities is significant. For sales, these go beyond the simple KPIs of inputs (# of calls made, # of appointments booked) and get to more serious outcomes, such as progress made towards revenue and actual revenue booked, measurements that reveal achievement, not just activity.

For the "broken rung" issue in sales, the role of the sales manager is critical, as it is in onboarding and retaining sales reps. Top sales insights point to the importance of training managers to become better coaches. But are your managers also being trained and coached on the idea of style and sales approach differences? Many women point to their sales manager as being a barrier to their success rather than an ally. You need to be vigilant that sales managers are being fair and impartial in their assessments and feedback.

Of course, not all sales reps start out in inside sales as an SDR, and not every sales rep wants to be promoted into sales management. That's why it's important for women to know what their opportunities are for growth within the sales organization – and research backs this up. Are there opportunities to grow into more lucrative or more challenging territories, product lines, or industry specialties? Opportunities to move up from door opening to closing? To move into higher ticket sales? To join a sales team working on key accounts or dedicated accounts? Sales managers can help their reps understand what's possible.

The third requirement, to reward outstanding performance while managing "converging" performance, may be the biggest challenge. The suggestion was that most of the people in your employ will perform towards the mean, and therefore their rewards should not vary too much from one another. But for outstanding performance, there should be much bigger rewards above the norm. Nonrecurring bonuses and "spot" awards were suggested. Along with rewards, opportunities to demonstrate outstanding performance are equally important.

Readiness for promotion also requires that women get exposed to the breadth and depth of experience that their male counterparts have.

That's where mentorship and sponsorship can be critical to career success. Sponsorship differs from mentorship in that mentors advise and sponsors advocate, so I consider them separately.

Provide Mentorship Opportunities

It is important that women in sales roles and in early leadership roles have the opportunity for mentorship. For my purposes, a mentor is a more experienced person within a company, team, or subject area who works with a newer, less experienced person, often referred to as a mentee. A good mentor will help their mentee develop strengths, learn from other's mistakes, and offer ideas and support. Often a mentor learns over time that they, too, have learned from the mentee, and it can be a mutually beneficial business relationship. A major study of its mentorship program at Sun Microsystems found that people with mentors were five times more likely to be promoted than those without mentors.[21]

The seven-year program, which involved pairing almost 1,000 employees with almost that many mentors, also improved employee retention at a rate that translated to a cost savings of $6.7 million to Sun! Another unexpected outcome was the remarkable benefits to the mentors, who were retained and promoted at even higher rates than their mentees.

There are more formal mentor/mentee relationships, and there are less formal ones. After hosting and moderating many sales leadership panels, I have found that most women don't want to be assigned a mentor. They would prefer to choose someone appropriate to their needs. Some companies match a more experienced woman rep to a new woman rep. But just because they are both women doesn't mean they will hit it off in a mentorship relationship. A better system is to facilitate ways for your sales reps to find a mentor if they would like to have one.

For example, a newer sales rep may not understand how to read a P&L statement, something that could benefit them in selling to their buyer. Asking someone in finance or a business leader at the company to teach them about P&Ls is a specific and quantifiable ask. That may lead to a broader mentorship relationship.

Mentoring alone, however, is insufficient to move women along the leadership path. Women need to be at the senior executive level in your organization in order for newer hires to see their potential future. If your organization already has multiple senior women leaders, then you have role models! Be sure your high-potential women reps and junior managers have opportunities to meet them, either in person or in large settings, or in video conferences. But if you are short on women leaders, it is all the more important to move women along that path.

Find Sponsors for High-Potential Women

Sponsorship is the best way to ensure that women are moving into senior positions in your organization. A sponsor is a more senior person in the organization (or outside of it) in a position of power who can be an advocate, someone who will recommend someone in a closed-door meeting or provide inside knowledge of opportunities. Most decisions are made in companies when only the leaders are in the room. The idea of a sponsor is that there is someone who will suggest Mary instead of Joe for that next promotion. When someone pushes back and says, "I don't think Mary is ready," that person speaks up and says that she is, offering reasons why. That's sponsorship in action. Some of us find sponsors on our own, and others get matched up. Either way, both men and women are fast-tracked by having a sponsor or two in an organization.

Some companies make a point of introducing sales reps to opportunities for mentorship and sponsorship by hosting one or more meetings on the topic. Leaders who are willing to mentor explain how to find a mentor, what the mentor/mentee relationship entails, and what a newer employee can expect from that relationship.

But a sponsor needs to really know the person, believe in her, and want to go the extra mile to push her career forward. A sponsor's relationship is deeper and perhaps more long-term. The sponsor may not be inside the sales team and must be someone with real clout inside the organization. It could also be someone in a partner or peer company who is respected at the company the woman seeking a sponsor works for.

Sales leaders can do a great deal to see that high-potential women on their teams are gaining the experience and opportunities they need in order to be promoted. Through a variety of experiences, they are more likely to find a sponsor. Here are some ways you can help:

- Make the option for mentors possible through a formal program or by allotting time for mentors and mentees to meet, or simply make introductions for this purpose
- Encourage women on your team to track their successes and step up even if they feel they are not ready yet. Put opportunities in front of them; let them know what's possible
- Identify high-potential reps for future leadership and sponsor them when opportunities arise
- Give high-potential female reps external opportunities such as Women Sales Pros Executive Presence sessions or #GirlsClub leadership training
- Tell a woman on your team about the potential you see in her – she may very well not see it herself

Leaders make all the difference, and some women are stepping up to leadership on their own through the creation of company-supported women in sales groups.

LucidChart helped women on their sales team launch Utah Women in Sales,[22] a thriving not-for-profit organization that is making a real difference initially throughout the state, now virtually – and reflecting well on the initial sponsor company. Once the pandemic hit, the organization went virtual and now has women and men from around North America attending their events.

Undoubtedly, many more support groups will be formed as more women are hired into sales organizations. But if you are hiring the first one or two into your organization, be sure that you also take responsibility for fairness in the path to promotion for the great women that you have worked so hard to attract, hire, onboard, and retain.

Now that I've given you the playbook that helps you attract, hire and retain more women in sales, let's discuss how to build a magnetic sales culture.

TOP **10** TIPS
TO PROMOTE WOMEN

1. Have a solid process in place to regularly teach about allyism

2. Enroll high-potential women into unique programs such as #GirlsClub and Women Sales Pros to support leadership development

3. Learn what other companies are doing internally

4. Identify non-typical "high potential" reps and let them know you believe they have potential

5. Let them know what specifically they need to work on to gain a promotion

6. Hold sales promotion conversations – a quarterly lunch, for example – with groups of sellers to be more transparent.

7. Recognize and share internally that your company has gender imbalance and share your commitment to inclusivity

8. Realize women look at your website before engaging, so sell your beliefs and vision there

9. Work so that 3rd party websites are sharing that you are an inclusive sales organization- or if not, fix it

10. Create flexible work schedules and continued remote work for those who can perform well remotely and need the flexibility, and ensure that remote workers are able to be judged equally to those in the office

CHAPTER EIGHT

Create a Great Sales Culture

"I alone cannot change the world, but I can cast a stone across the waters to create many ripples."

MOTHER TERESA

It is possible and doable to create a great, magnetic sales culture that pulls prospective hires your way and helps you build a dynamic company. If you are someone who has the traits to be (or has been a) change maker in your organization, whether a company leader or sales leader, you can do this!

There are many great examples of companies that have worked hard to:

- Show up with a strong mission and vision
- Lead by example
- Hire thoughtfully and inclusively
- Do whatever it takes for success

By identifying what IS working and who IS leading the way, we can find mentors, examples, and insights which lead us to build those inclusive teams with a top sales culture.

From the companies I've been around over the past 30+ years, a great sales culture is one that starts at the top. Sales culture is creating a safe space for everyone on the team where they can feel seen and heard and can make a positive impact. It is intentional.

How do you know you have a good sales culture? You ask your team members regularly. It is like the difference between diversity and inclusion. One is a "check the box" (diversity), and the other is assimilating everyone to become an important part of the team (inclusion). It is not enough to say you have a good culture within your sales team. It is regular action that makes your team one that is supportive, creative, and successful for all.

Show Up with a Strong Mission and Vision

Henry Schuck is the founder and CEO of Zoominfo (Nasdaq: ZI), with more than 30,000 customers. Early on, however, when Henry was CEO and Co-founder of DiscoverOrg, he realized that women didn't even apply for sales positions at his startup, and he wanted to change that. My advice to him at the time was to try new and different ideas to attract non-traditional candidates (other than young white males) for sales roles and to "try harder" within his process. Not long after that, he had the opportunity to hire Carolyn Murray as his first female SDR. She turned the opportunity down initially, so Henry "tried harder" and got his head of sales at the time to invite Carolyn to come back for one more conversation.

Carolyn was about to accept an administrative position elsewhere, so they encouraged her to try a sales role, if not at DiscoverOrg, then somewhere else, because they felt they saw her potential. Henry said he'd support Carolyn's success. Because of the extra encouragement, Carolyn ended up accepting the SDR role and became the fastest SDR to hit $1M ARR through her cold-calling efforts. Her success in that role, including hitting over 170% of the quota, led her to become their first female account executive.

DiscoverOrg went on to acquire its biggest competitor, ZoomInfo, and is the market leader in the SaaS data "single source of truth" space. Carolyn has been an Enterprise Account Executive with ZoomInfo for nearly seven years and is a leader in sales success in the company.

If You Can't Find It, Create It

When a rapidly growing software-as-a-service company is moving as fast as a rocket, it is difficult to find diverse sales leader candidates, even when leadership agrees that building inclusive sales teams is the right strategy. Such was the case for Outreach, the category leader in Sales Execution with over 1,200 employees.

The CRO at the time, Anna Baird, put the word out to find women sales leaders to interview for open leadership roles. They didn't have much luck, even with internal recruiters and outside agency support. Anna partnered with SVP, People & Organizational Development Pamela Mattsson to design and launch a program to grow diverse talent from within. Female sales leaders were nominated from across the sales organization to participate in the nine-month program. Leadership made it clear that the participants did not "owe" Outreach anything. Should they end up wanting to move on to another company, the industry would be better for it. They also positioned the inaugural participants as co-designers, empowering them to give real-time feedback to shape the learning experience.

The cohort of participants met monthly and engaged in topics such as leadership brand, visibility, influence, managing up and developing down, strategic thinking, storytelling, and giving back. External and internal speakers shared insights and expertise on topics ranging from navigating career journeys as a woman in sales (it's impossible to do it all, and it's okay to ask for help), building your authentic brand, and elevating thought leadership. The program culminated in a capstone presentation to the Executive Leadership team in which participants were asked to find an issue/problem within their segment with no clear owner and prepare a creative solution that was executive-level ready, compelling, data-driven, and powerful.

"Women hold only 12% of coveted top sales jobs in the industry. We want to interrupt that at Outreach with the RISE program," Pamela says. "RISE stands for Recognize, Inspire, Support, and Engage, and is a nine-month long program to elevate women in sales and give them the community, visibility, and tangible skills to advance in their careers. The program has nine focal areas, which we roll out over a nine-month period of time. It spans topics from owning your career aspirations to strategic thinking."

The Outreach program focuses on developing others and giving back to the community. Its RISE graduates become future mentors for other exceptional women in sales. This was the inaugural year of the program, and participants were engaged as co-designers, providing feedback along the way to shape their program and what will follow. "We know this first iteration was not perfect and will use feedback to enhance the program for future groups," Pamela says. "The biggest shared takeaway for program designers and participants was that, above all else, creating a community of talented female sales leaders to connect, create, and collaborate, was priceless. If you want to know what your diverse sales talent needs to be successful, ask them, and then take action to build what they need WITH them."

Here's what a RISE participant said:

"We talked a lot in the program about being 'the only' and how often we are the only female voice in the room. The most common challenge for women in sales is finding allies, and more importantly, advocates—people who will invest in you and elevate your voice," the woman says.

"RISE did just that. At a high level, the program reminded me of the importance of taking time for my own development and the value of stepping back from the day-to-day, especially as I move higher and have more responsibility. I understand that I am not alone in the challenges that I face as a female in business- others feel the same way. Most importantly, I learned that much of the way I approach my work is not 'being different,' it is being authentic, and my methods constitute thought leadership and best practice for leading a more diverse sales workforce with more diverse buyers."

While Outreach is just getting started, it just graduated its first cohort of female sales leaders, two of which were promoted during the process. The second RISE program will leverage learnings from the first and is being expanded to other diverse populations.

Lead By Example

Ryan Bott, Global VP of Revenue at Sodexo, is responsible for over $1B in annual revenue and four centers of sales and marketing around the globe. He raises his hand and agrees to be on a virtual (or, in past years, in-person) panel to discuss what being an ally for women in sales and for diversity, and inclusion is all about.

When asked, Ryan will thoughtfully come up with questions and angles to add his perspective as a male leader. On one panel, he shared with the audience how reporting to an African-American female executive altered his own viewpoint on how he thinks about female colleagues and people of color being an "only" or one of a few on a team. He fields questions from other male leaders and generously offers his time and perspective. Ryan could easily say he is too busy, and no one would fault him, but he shows up time and time again. It is so important for male allies to do this so that, as a woman, I'm not talking in an echo chamber to other women. When male leaders get into the conversation, we have more of an opportunity for change.

Hire thoughtfully and inclusively

Many tech leaders have told me they don't have the time to find a balanced slate of sales candidates; they just hire the best person in front of them. This perpetuates the same old hiring adage and has kept giving us the male-majority sales world we've all come to know. By building a pipeline over time, with enough different inputs to create a flow of candidates, you can build an inclusive sales team. Is it hard? Yes. Does it fluctuate in terms of more candidates sometimes and fewer other times? Yes. As we've been moving through the reimagination of work in late 2022 and early 2023, we're seeing massive job and career changes going on due to possibilities never before imagined and an emphasis on mental wellness plus quality-of-life issues. It may feel like a losing battle sometimes to have quality candidates that can allow you to build an inclusive team.

Do whatever it takes for success

The only way you'll be successful is if the top of the organization is committed to making this happen. It is not unlike any other change issue. I'll use sales training as an example. When we ask managers to hold their sales reps accountable, and it doesn't happen, upper leadership steps in to remind managers of the commitment to success. When the going gets tough, it is natural to drop the hard things and go with what the default actions are. Creating dynamic, creative, inclusive sales teams means a shift in thinking, and it also means a shift (for the better) in the marketplace and within your organization. You can do this.

At Score More Sales, we use an acronym, "Try-Do," in sessions with sales leaders and company leaders on ways to gain understanding as we all sometimes stumble to say the right things and move forward in a more inclusive way:

T Talk about solutions
R Respond for understanding
Y Yield the urge to simply "fix" a situation
D Dare to make a difference
O Offer ideas, challenges, and lessons learned

Our companies need more of us to hold a conversation when we don't have all of the answers, and it might be uncomfortable. In the cancel culture world we live in today, some folks are just too fearful that they will say the wrong thing, even when they are trying to learn.

I saw recently on LinkedIn where a man posted a comment about how he felt that most women really don't want a B2B sales position, and that's why there are so many men in sales roles. A couple of women quickly told him how wrong he was, and it shut the conversation down. The next time that happens around you use the "Try-Do" formula and have a conversation. Don't bring all of the answers. Instead, ask twice as many questions. Ask tough questions and good questions. Bring curiosity and leave with a new perspective.

If we all can be a little less sure of the "right answer" and more open to seeing another perspective, it can transform our work environments, especially the sales team.

Many female sales candidates and BIPOC sales candidates look at your websites and look you up on 3rd party sites to learn what you have done for inclusion, and they will be asking you questions. It is challenging to come into a sales team as an "only" – the only woman, or only woman in that region, or the only person of color.

I interviewed a woman on the Women Sales Pros "Conversations with Women in Sales" podcast recently who looked at over 30 companies when job searching and had six companies interested in hiring her in an account exec role. She ruled out several because there was no commitment to inclusion and no plan in place to make change happen. She saw no evidence on their website or from initial questions that received blank-stare answers. It's too bad for the several she quickly ruled out because at the company she did join, she hit the ground running. In her fourth month, she was 50% ahead of her goal.

Let's Do This Together

You are not alone here. I offer several pages of resources, including articles, podcasts, women in sales groups, and educational programs and books, that you may find helpful in your quest for a more inclusive sales team.

TOP **10** TIPS

TO ELEVATE YOUR EFFORTS FOR MORE WOMEN IN SALES

1. Become a champion for change, and embrace being uncomfortable at times

2. Widen your horizons

3. Take steps every day to move forward

4. Learn from others

5. Share your successes

6. Ask powerful questions like, "How are we doing?"

7. Be open to others' points of view

8. Start with small steps – then go bigger

9. Shake up the norm – create a new norm

10. Let's do this together!

ABOUT LORI RICHARDSON

In my early twenties, my first profession as an adult was teaching young children at a childcare center on the University of Washington campus in Seattle, WA. It was a low-paying role, even for those with advanced degrees.

I became a single parent after leaving a physically abusive marriage, and suddenly the enjoyable, rewarding work I was doing just didn't pay enough for me as head of a household.

It was perplexing to figure out what to do. Where could I make the same money as my male counterparts and find personal reward in the work?

There was a nontraditional jobs program for women happening on a series of ten Saturdays, so I found Saturday childcare through a friend and signed up. During the program, I learned how to build scaffolding, pour cement, complete finish carpentry, and assorted other blue-collar jobs. On one Saturday, someone came in and talked about technology. I was smitten by the idea of working in tech and making a good living.

Initially, I focused on building the technology, and since I'm such a people person, working with technology in a warehouse type of setting was not going to work for me. That was a wrong move. I recalled the great upbringing I had working for my grandmother, Mimi, in her women's apparel store, and finally put two-and-two together to go from making technology to selling technology.

My timing was great because, in the early 1980s, a revolution was happening in business to decentralize large business computing onto personal computers.

The first job I took was with a regional computer store, Byte Shops NW. I was afraid to leave a low-paying but steady salary for my new sales role, which paid straight commission. What that meant was that other than a small draw, I had to sell to survive. There were mouths to feed, not just mine, and our future depended on how quickly I ramped up and how successful I was.

Looking back, I have no doubt that the need made me focus and grind it out until I succeeded. It didn't hurt, though, that companies had a big appetite for the new computing power, and we had great sales training through manufacturers like IBM, Hewlett-Packard, Apple, Xerox, and others. It was the perfect time to learn and ramp up.

Fast forward to today. I've had my own firm, Score More Sales, since 2002. In 2015, I was suddenly struck by the number of clients I was working with who had all-male sales teams or teams with only one or two women. There were few women VPs of Sales, CROs, or women in other sales executive roles.

And as I write now, in 2023, it sometimes still feels like the 1980s. Where are the women in sales? Where are the women sales reps? Where are the women sales managers? The female sales VPs? The CROs? They are still too few and far between. We lost women in sales during the pandemic. This realization continues for me, and thus my journey to understand more about and help solve this business puzzle.

In addition to running Score More Sales, a sales strategy firm for mid-market companies who want to fix sales team issues, I have grown my involvement and commitment to increasing the number of women in sales.

Six years ago, my dear friend and mentor Jill Konrath handed over the leadership of her group of women sales experts to me. Shortly after, I rebranded the group to *Women Sales Pros* and added a mission and vision of increasing the number of women in sales and sales leadership roles. I created the She Sells Summit to bring all of the groups helping women in sales together so we can share our successes and support one another. I also host Conversations with Women in Sales, a podcast where I interview sales pros monthly to inspire women and men to improve their selling skills.

My advice and lessons come from a very successful 20-year career in tech, financial, and distribution sales and sales leadership positions with companies like Apple and Thomson Reuters. I am regularly listed as a sales influencer, am a sought-after speaker, was named one of LinkedIn's "Top Voices in Sales" in 2018, have been a Sales Influencer for Salesforce in 2021 and 2022, and I received a "Lifetime Achievement Award" for my work with women in sales from AA-ISP (an organization for the inside sales profession) in 2019. All that aside, I've had hundreds of amazing conversations with women wanting to get into a career like B2B sales and women in sales careers having one challenge or another. This has proven to be so rewarding for me that I can't imagine not continuing this mission – even if it sometimes seems untenable.

ABOUT WOMEN SALES PROS

Women Sales Pros is a community consisting of a group of female top sales experts, which recently launched a bigger community for those interested in building, supporting, or just belonging to inclusive sales teams. Our vision is to support all of the groups, organizations, clubs, and events that support bringing more women into B2B sales and sales leadership. Reach out at: https://womensalespros.com/

Follow us on Twitter and Instagram @womensalespros

Join us on our Women Sales Pros LinkedIn page

https://www.linkedin.com/company/women-sales-pros/

Listen to the Podcast "Conversations with Women in Sales" on iTunes, Stitcher, or YouTube.

https://womensalespros.com/podcast/

(Bonus points for sharing it with a woman in sales OR giving us a 5-star review on iTunes)

Follow the She Sells Summit website for past event recorded sessions and future events.

ENDNOTES

[1] https://www.gartner.com/smarterwithgartner/why-sales-must-hire-more-women/

[2] report (https://discoverorg.com/blog/gender-diversity-bench-mark-2019/)

[3] https://www.linkedin.com/pulse/how-women-break-rules-selling-yet-still-outperformmen-chris-orlob/

[4] https://www.xactlycorp.com/resources/guides/2019-state-of-gender-equality-in-sales

[5] https://www.linkedin.com/pulse/supersalesman-wondersaleswoman-jo%C3%ABl-le-bon-ph-d-/

[6] https://hbr.org/2014/08/why-women-dont-apply-for-jobs-unless-theyre-100-qualified?referral=03759&cm_vc=rr_item_page.bottom.

[7] https://www.theladders.com/career-advice/job-descriptions-driv-ing-away-women

[8] https://discoverorg.com/blog/selling-sales-to-women/

[9] https://www.linkedin.com/posts/kariannabarreto_utdsales-whoosh-ac-tivity-6590653958975479808-dFeW

[10] Mikki Hebl, Christine L. Nittrouer, Abigail R. Corrington, Juan M. Madera. https://hbr.org/2018/09/how-we-describe-male-and-fe-male-job-applicants-differently?referral=03759&cm_vc=rr_item_page.bottom]

[11] Stefanie K. Johnson, David R. Hekman, Elsa T. Chan. https://hbr.org/2016/04/if-theres-only-one-woman-in-your-candidate-pool-theres-statistically-no-chance-shell-be-hired

[12] https://www.devinegroup.com/uncategorized/traits-of-a-hunter/

[13] https://www.pewsocialtrends.org/interactives/strong-men-caring-women/

[14] https://www.peaksalesrecruiting.com/blog/succeed-female-sales/

[15] https://www.brainshark.com/sites/default/files/2017-cso-insights-sales-manager-enablement-report.pdf

[16] https://www.mckinsey.com/~/media/McKinsey/Featured%20Insights/Gender%20Equality/Women%20in%20the%20Workplace%202019/Women-in-the-workplace-2019.ashx

[17] https://leanin.org/women-in-the-workplace/2019

[18] https://www.mckinsey.com/featured-insights/diversity-and-inclusion/women-in-the-workplace

[19] https://www.amazon.com/Sales-Development-Playbook-Repeatable-Accelerate-ebook/dp/B01AOG3N7Q/ref=tmm_kin_swatch_0?_encoding=UTF8&qid=&sr=

[20] https://www.mckinsey.com/featured-insights/diversity-and-inclusion/women-in-the-workplace

[21] https://knowledge.wharton.upenn.edu/article/workplace-loyalties-change-but-the-value-of-mentoring-doesnt/

[22] https://www.utahwomeninsales.com/

RESOURCES

Earlier in the book, a resource was mentioned to help teach about recognizing and removing bias in the corporate world. I have used this with great success, and at publication time, they still offer a free download to the tools:

50 Ways to Fight Bias: A training activity that helps you combat gender bias at work from LeanIn

Also Recommended:

Shared Sisterhood: How to Take Collective Action for Racial and Gender Equity at Work
Tina Opie, Beth A. Livingston

Don't Fix Women: The Practical Path to Gender Equality at Work
Joy Burnford, Denise Williams

Books About Sales and Revenue Growth, Written by Women Sales Pros and Sales Experts

30 Days to Sales Success
Meridith Elliott Powell

Thrive
Meridith Elliott Powell

Winning in the Trust and Value Economy
Meridith Elliott Powell

How Good Humans Sell: The Proven Path to B2B Sales Success
Catherine Brown

The Sales Development Playbook
Trish Bertuzzi

Value Propositions that Sell:
Turning Your Message into a Magnet That Attracts Buyers
Lisa D. Dennis

The Modern Seller
Amy Franko

Heart and Sell: 10 Universal Truths Every Salesperson Needs to Know
Shari Levitin

Beat the Bots: How Your Humanity Can Future-proof
Your Tech Sales Career
Anita Nielsen

Biz Dev Done Right: Demystifying the Sales Process and Achieving
the Results You Want
Caryn Kopp & Carl Gould

Side B: Remix Your Leadership Style
Paula S. White

Journey to the Top: How to Reach Your Peak Performance Life
Jamie Crosbie

Pick Up the Damn Phone!
Joanne S. Black

The Inside Sales Solution
Nancy Calabrese

Fix Your Business
Melinda F. Emerson

Become Your Own Boss in 12 Months
Melinda Emerson

Look Me in the Eye
Julie Hansen

Act Like A Sales Pro
Julie Hansen

Sales Presentations for Dummies
Julie Hansen

The Top Sales Leader Playbook: How to Win 5x Deals Repeatedly
Lisa D. Magnuson

The Top Seller Advantage: Powerful Strategies to Build Long-Term Executive Relationships
Lisa D. Magnuson

Selling to Big Companies
Jill Konrath

Snap Selling
Jill Konrath

Agile Selling
Jill Konrath

More Sales, Less Time
Jill Konrath

Whale Hunting With Global Accounts
Barbara Weaver Smith

Whale Hunting
Tom Searcy & Barbara Weaver Smith

No More Cold Calling
Joanne S. Black

Predictable Revenue
Marylou Tyler and Jeremey Donovan

Predictable Prospecting
Aaron Ross & Marylou Tyler

Conversations That Sell:
Collaborate with Buyers and Make Every Conversation Count
Nancy Bleeke

The Art of Commercial Conversations
Bernadette McClelland

The Best Sales Book Ever/The Best Sales Leadership Ever
Connie Podesta & Meridith Elliott Powell

Emotional Intelligence for Sales Leadership:
The Secret to Building High Performance Sales Teams
Colleen Stanley

Emotional Intelligence for Sales Success:
Connect with Customers and Get Results
Colleen Stanley

The Field Guide to Sales
Debbie Mrazek

The Sales Magnet: How to Get More Customers Without Cold Calling
Kendra Lee

Selling Against the Goal:
How Corporate Sales Professionals Generate the Leads they Need
Kendra Lee

Go for No: Yes is the Destination, No is How You Get There
Andrea Waltz & Richard Fenton

Books About Sales and Revenue Growth, Written by Women

Love Your Team: A Survival Guide for Sales Managers in a Hybrid World
Helen Fanucci

Right on the Money: New Principles for Bold Growth
Colleen Francis

Nonstop Sales Boom:
Powerful Strategies to Drive Consistent Growth Year over Year
Colleen Francis

Selling with Noble Purpose – 2nd Edition:
How to Drive Revenue and Do Work that Makes You Proud
Lisa Earle McLeod

Leading with Noble Purpose: How to Create a Tribe of True Believers
Lisa Earle McLeod

Heels to Deals: How Women are Dominating in Business-to-Business Sales
Heidi Solomon-Orlick, Editor

Heart-Powered Sales:
Grow Your Sales Exponentially with Emotional Intelligence and Intuition
Robin Treasure

Selling from Your Comfort Zone: The Power of Alignment Marketing
Stacey Hall

Work It, Girl:
A Modern-Day Career Guide for Women in Sales (book and sales planner)
Tania Doub

Quit: The Power of Knowing When to Walk Away
Annie Duke

Thinking in Bets:
Making Smarter Decisions When you Don't Have all the Facts
Annie Duke

Be Unexpected: Resetting Routines to Revolutionize the Future of Work
Marva Bailer

Embrace Your Edge:
Pave Your Own Path as an Immigrant Woman in the Workplace
Hang Thi Yen Black

Top Podcasts Hosted or Co-Hosted by Women about Sales and Revenue Growth

https://womensalespros.com/sales/the-top-new-sales-podcasts-hosted-by-women/

https://womensalespros.com/leadership/top-33-sales-podcasts-hosted-or-co-hosted-by-women/

Organizations, Communities, and Groups Focused on More Women in B2B Sales

Blog post: https://womensalespros.com/leadership/we-need-each-other/

Women Sales Pros: https://womensalespros.com/

She Sells Summit: https://shesellssummit.com/

Made in the USA
Las Vegas, NV
30 January 2023

66507340R00057